Realizing **empathy**

Realizing
empathy

*An Inquiry into
the Meaning of Making*

SEUNG CHAN LIM

Eames Century Modern by House Industries, Din Next Ultra Light Condensed, Din Next Light Condensed, **Din Next Condensed**, Din Next Light, **Din Next Medium**, *Centaur MT Std Bold Italic*, and Bell Centennial Std by Linotype, 나눔명조 by NHN.

Offset printing, hard cover and smyth sewn binding by Hyosung Moonhwa.

Designed and illustrated by Seung Chan Lim.
Chief edited by Todd Sattersten.
Copy edited by Leslie Fisher.

Copyright © 2013 Seung Chan Lim

All rights reserved.

First published in 2013.

This first edition is made possible in full by support from the generous Kickstarter backers.

The first draft of this book was produced in partial fulfillment of the requirements for the degree Master of Fine Arts in Graphic Design in the department of Graphic Design of the Rhode Island School of Design, Providence, RI.

To contact the author or to order additional copies, please visit http://realizingempathy.com/

Publisher's Cataloging-In-Publication Data
(Prepared by The Donohue Group, Inc.)

Lim, Seung Chan.

   Realizing empathy : an inquiry into the meaning of making / Seung Chan Lim. — 1st ed.

     p. : ill. ; cm.

   Issued also as an ebook.
   Includes bibliographical references.
   ISBN: 978-0-9858846-0-4

   1. Art—Psychology. 2. Empathy. 3. User-centered system design. 4. Creative ability. I. Title.

N71 .L55 2013   701/.15

FOREWORD	*vii*
DEDICATION	*xv*
ACKNOWLEDGEMENTS	*xxvi*
PREFACE	*xxxiii*

	2
	20
	68
	88
DIARY	*116*
	216
INTRODUCTION	*7*
	254
	258
PROLOGUE	*25*
	280
	304

INTERVIEW	*40*
EMPATHY	*73*
REALIZING EMPATHY	*95*
MAKING AND EMPATHY	*121*
FACILITATING EMPATHY	*221*
DESIGN AND EMPATHY	*263*
EPILOGUE	*285*
AFTERWORD	*311*
CONVERSATIONS	*322*
BIBLIOGRAPHY	*327*
SPECIAL NOTE	*344*

FOREWORD

Seung Chan has given us more than deep thought and deeper feeling for the practice of design in our still-new century.

Realizing Empathy signals a long-needed transition from technocratic paradigm to human bias. I say "paradigm" because that term makes conscious that we do not know what we do not know. We cannot see how possibilities are constricted by our current beliefs in what technology offers, nor in what it tends to take away. And I say "bias" because humanism is a prejudice that we should want. To want anything else is simply inhumane.

Yet Seung Chan's work is more than a signal. It is a humanistic map of a territory sensitively explored by an individual who made his own transition from technology-focused to relationship-focused interactions. Technology in the presence of our biology will always be disappointing—by its nature it cannot be as transparent and effective as we want. To be sane is to want technology only insofar as it serves us, our needs, and our desires. Do we want a world in which technology has its own wants, even metaphorically? *Realizing Empathy* answers powerfully that we can and ought to have what we want.

The rising participation of capital-D "Design" in the evolution of products and services may be confusing us about how

PAUL

FOREWORD

far we've come. For example, we may think programmers are no longer in control because they stand shoulder-to-shoulder with "communication designers" or "interaction designers." Yet we do not have a rigorous, yet subjective, prescriptive, yet expansive methodology for designing the contexts in which we as "persons," not "users," may be our own designers. We have some distance to go.

As Humberto Maturana has explained and Hugh Dubberly has modeled, "metadesign" is what designers must now do. As metadesigners, we enable us all to become what we want to become. In other words, to be designers of our own worlds. To do less is to place technology—that is, any instrumentality—more in control of outcomes than our desires. It is not for want of technology that we cannot design our own world, it is for want of technique. And in that vacuum, code and computation hold sway.

Realizing Empathy offers us clear waypoints to metadesign. Few individuals have the courage to be a guide in such a territory. As a highly experienced software designer and coder, Seung Chan has the authority to declaim that users and computers are in an "abusive relationship." These are strong words in an era dominated by the computational triumphs of software giants that control the way we find products to consume, find our friends and preferences, find our way. But he could feel the gap between effective code and effective conversation. As a highly disciplined practitioner, he knew he had to understand "materiality" even when crafting bits and not atoms. Though his path is steeped in the immateriality of goals and desires, the whole journey is about being biological creatures, being human, being inextricably physical/material and social/relational at the same time.

I believe that profound insight—seeing with new eyes—can only come from a singular viewpoint that defines a limitation and feels a passion, and then holds an obsession until limitation is overcome. The drive to improve comes from a place of pain and moves to relief, not vice-versa. The author could not have started at the Rhode Island School of Design (RISD) and then gone to, say, the Massachusetts Institute of Technology (MIT). Today's design education does not give a language to the limits of technology; nor do temples of the technocratic paradigm have an answer for the problems they create.

Ironically, reaching grounded and powerful innovation demands a rigorous systemic approach—as we would expect from engineering—as well as a new language of expression—as we would expect from design. Seung Chan has developed a new language system that brings coherence to his humanistic cosmos. Like all who venture to create

FOREWORD

a new cosmos, a new semantic space of possibilities, his biggest obstacle is that of being misunderstood. Disruptive ideas, expressed in the new language they require, will always feel uncomfortable or dangerous because they create uncertainty, which creates personal cost. But by crafting interpersonal stories and visual exemplars of his own journey, he gives us his energy and his heart.

Through discipline, craft, and caring, Seung Chan has earned the right to ask us to listen. His models bridge listening to empathy. Our world of design, and our world, need his work.

Paul Pangaro[1]
January 2, 2013

[1] Dr. Paul Pangaro's career spans product strategy, prescriptive innovation, and organizational dynamics, with roles as technology executive, professor of cybernetics, entrepreneur, and performer. Through prototyping, lecturing, and writing, Paul's career has focused on the cognitive and social needs of human beings. He has taught at Stanford University and School of the Visual Arts in New York, and has lectured on his approach to conversation software in North America, Europe, and Brazil.

DEDICATION

Today marks the fifth year anniversary

DEDICATION

of Dr. Randy Pausch's "Last Lecture."[1]

To most people, the lecture was likely to have been nothing but a wave of inspiration.

But for me,
it has a rather somber association.

In college, Randy saved my life by giving me a reason to study computer science. For the generation when education itself was considered luxury, it is perhaps strange to think that one needs a reason to study something. But to be completely honest, without a clear reason, or a sense of purpose, retaining interest in computer science was a struggle. If there was anything that kept me going, it was a sense of pride and duty. After all, computer science was what Carnegie Mellon University was best known for, and it is what I had promised my parents I would be studying.

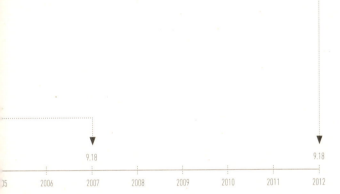

[1] On September 18, 2007, computer science professor Randy Pausch stepped in front of an audience of 400 people at Carnegie Mellon University to deliver a last lecture called "Really Achieving Your Childhood Dreams." With slides of his CT scans beaming out to the audience, Randy told his audience about the cancer that was devouring his pancreas and that would claim his life in a matter of months. On the stage that day, Randy was youthful, energetic, handsome, often cheerfully, darkly funny. He seemed invincible. But this was a brief moment, as he himself acknowledged. Randy's lecture became a phenomenon, as has the book he wrote based on the same principles, celebrating the dreams we all strive to make realities. Sadly, Randy lost his battle to pancreatic cancer on July 25, 2008. His legacy will continue to inspire us all, for generations to come. (The Last Lecture, 2008, "Home")

That was,
until I took Randy's class.

What I learned in Randy's class was that I didn't have to be interested in computer science to learn computer science. According to Randy, all I had to be interested in was sharing with others such feelings as joy, sorrow, surprise, or even fear. For him, computer science was nothing more than a means to that end. It was a medium for empathy.

And that
resonated with me.
Profoundly.

And just like that, I had finally found the reason to study computer science.

1995　1996　1997　1998　1999　2000　2001　2002　2003

Freshman　Sophomore　Junior　Senior

But then I lost touch with Randy. *For eight years.*

As a matter of fact, it wasn't until a month before his last lecture, that I sent him the following e-mail:

I don't know if you remember me. My name is Slim from your BVW² class from way back in 1999. I worked on the Van Gogh project. I've been working at MAYA Design for the past eight years!

I now serve as the assistant director of engineering here, and we're looking to hire some hardcore thinkers who are also genius makers.

I thought ETC would be full of such people! Are you the right person to talk to if I want to figure out how to lure that talent over? Are there protocols for doing such a thing? (i.e., hold an informal info session at ETC)

Any advice would be awesome.

Thanks!

Slim

2006 2007

8.15

To which he responded:

Slim,

Good to hear from you, and *of course* I remember you —things like the Van Gogh world leave long memories!

I'm sure the ETC would love to have MAYA come and recruit— and there are definitely venues for that. Unfortunately, I'm no longer involved in the day-to-day of the ETC, so I've CC'd Drew Davidson, who can help you out with things.

Best wishes,

Randy

I don't know if it's obvious, but I had no idea he was terminally ill. As a matter of fact, the subtext of my e-mail is that I was trying to show off to Randy that I had made significant advancements in my career since graduation.

[2] Building Virtual Worlds (BVW is a project-based course where inter-disciplinary teams will build virtual worlds and other interactive content. The course will emphasize the technical mechanics of how to build virtual worlds, but will also cover the basics of environmental design, interactive game design, non-linear storytelling, virtual reality, and interdisciplinary teamwork. The goal of Building Virtual Worlds (BVW) is to take students with varying talents, backgrounds, and perspectives and put them together to do what they couldn't do alone. This course has traditionally had students from art, architecture, design, drama, computer science, electrical and computer engineering, human-computer interaction, music, social sciences, and a few other majors. These disciplines all have different standards for how they communicate, how they train their students, and how they evaluate the quality of work. It is extremely important that students in this course be tolerant of the different cultures that are represented. Based on experiences in the real world with these kinds of interdisciplinary teams, one of our goals is "getting through the semester without a fistfight occurring in a group." (Klug, Schell, 2009, "The Class")

Why was I showing off to Randy? Because I wanted him to be proud of me. It is one of those **silly things we do** to those whom we love and admire.

Instead of just telling them that we love them or that they mean a great deal to us, we try to gain their recognition by bragging to them about something that is utterly meaningless in the grand scheme of things. And because we get so blinded by our desires to be recognized by the other, we fail to tell them what it is that we really mean to tell them, which is that we love them dearly.

When Randy told me that he was not involved in the day-to-day activities of the ETC, I was surprised, but I didn't think much of it. *As a matter of fact,* it wasn't until a couple weeks after his last lecture that I found out that he was terminally ill.

Guess how I found out about it?

By watching his lecture on the Web.

On   the   Web.

A lecture held just a few miles from where I worked.
I remember being completely awash in a sense of shame.

How could I have been so poor at keeping in touch with someone I considered **my hero?**

I tried blaming it on my shyness. I tried blaming it on my busy life. I tried all sorts of excuses before giving up, and quickly writing him a long e-mail pouring my heart out.

But then, as I hit the "send" button, I began to realize that at this point, his inbox was probably overflowing with e-mails in response to his last lecture. That perhaps he would never get to read my e-mail. That he may never know **that he saved my life.**

Staring into the computer screen, I couldn't help but ask *why?* Why couldn't I have told him sooner? How stupid does one have to be, to wait so long **to say something so simple?**

I really hope you don't make the same mistake I made.

_{It's one of the few regrets I have in my life.}

If you love someone, tell them.
Today.
No, do it now.
Right now.
Just a few simple words.

Thank you and I love you.

Do it for them. Do it for yourself. Because you deserve better. We all deserve better.

Thank you, Randy. I love you.
I dedicate this book in your name.

Seung Chan Lim
September 18, 2012

I opened the course to fifty undergraduates from all different
departments of the university. We had actors, English
majors and sculptors mixed with engineers, math majors,
and computer geeks. These were students whose paths
might never had reason to cross,
given how autonomous the various disciplines at Carnegie
Mellon could be. But we made these kids unlikely partners
with each other, forcing them to do together
what they couldn't do alone.
RANDY PAUSCH / COMPUTER SCIENTIST

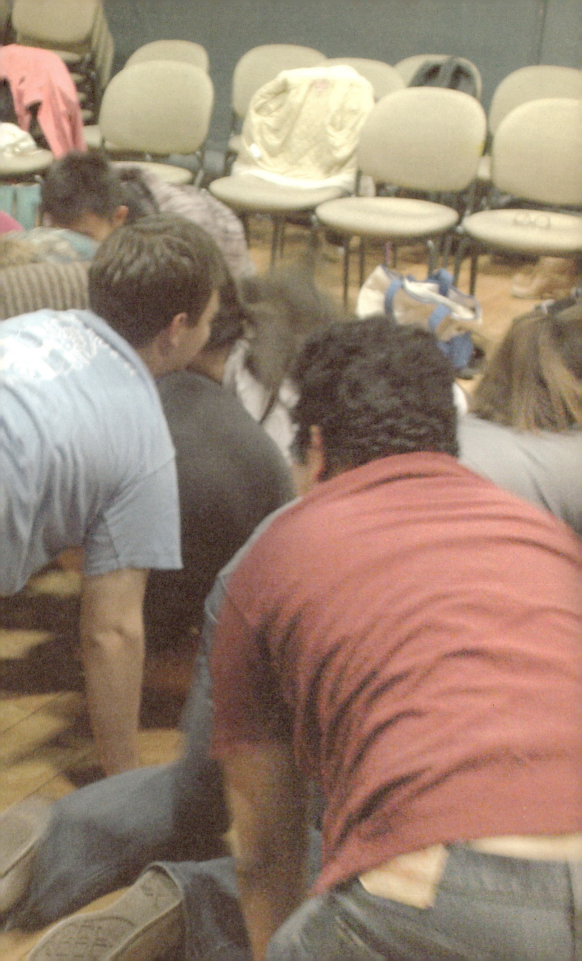

SLIM

It is a great honor to be able to say that the insights shared across these pages result from being around brilliant people rather than being in solitude. I would like to take a moment to thank some of the most influential minds that have helped shaped this book.

First of all, I'd like to thank my parents. The weekly conversations we've had on topics ranging from child education to death have been invaluable. I've always wanted to tell you that after spending many years trying to make the best choices in life, I have come to realize that I am most thankful for the one thing I didn't get to choose: you. 어머니, 아버지 진심으로 감사드립니다. 낳아주신 은혜 평생 잊지 않겠습니다.

I haven't the slightest clue how I will repay my debt to my three thesis advisers: David Gersten, Paul Pangaro, and Thomas Ockerse. Needless to say, the different perspectives you all have shared with me on topics ranging from semiotics to phenomenology to conversation theory have been invaluable. But above all, I cannot thank you enough for your trust and encouragement. You all have been incredibly generous with your time and patience. I am infinitely grateful for your generosity.

I would also like to extend my gratitude to An-Lon Chen, Anson Ann, David Watson, Jeff Wong, and Joonkoo Park

xxvii

for accompanying me from the very early stages of the first draft. Your insights and feedback have been invaluable in adding both depth and breadth to this book. You are living proof that empathic conversations can indeed take place online, even when the venue is Facebook or Posterous.

At both the Rhode Island School of Design (RISD) and Brown University, I was fortunate enough to have learned from those who exemplify the very act of listening in their teaching. In particular, I would like to thank Anne West, Chris Rose, Connie Crawford, Doug Scott, George Gordon, Peter Prip, and Tucker Houlihan for being so generous with your time, and responding to my seemingly endless chain of questions. It is amazing how much more I can learn from someone who listens.

A very special thanks goes out to the 2008 freshmen class section 20 and Alba Corrado who gave me the very opportunity to be amidst these brilliant young minds. I felt unbelievably lucky to have been with you all on the first day of graduate school. To this day, I cannot forget the valuable lessons I was able to glean from merely being in your presence. Stay beautiful, always.

A warm thanks to Yuki Kawae without whom my last year in graduate school would have been just dull. Thank you very much for taking interest in my thesis and inspiring me with your own stories. May the conversations live on in the Woodshop.

It is also with the deepest appreciation I say that the book you're now holding in your hands would not have been possible had it not been for the hard work of Todd Sattersten, our chief editor, and Leslie Fisher, our copy editor. They have read, challenged, and re-read each and every page to make sure that the book was held to the highest of standards. Any semblance of clarity and polish is due credit to these two remarkable individuals.

Finally, it is impossible to imagine whether I would have had the energy to pursue five years of relentlessness had it not been for Yong Joo Kim, who has stood by me with her sense of humor and positive attitude. Thank you and I love you. You inspire me like nobody I have ever known.

Seung Chan Lim
January 10, 2013

xxix

PREFACE

The school I attended as an undergraduate

was filled with an amazing roster of well-known computer science professors.

Whenever I mentioned their names to students of
computer science at other universities, they'd remark,
"Wow! You're studying under that professor?
That's amazing!
Did you know that he invented the algorithm for ____?"

Unfortunately,
what I learned from most of them, was actually quite
minimal.

As a matter of fact, I was more confused about
computer science after having taken their classes.

This is not to point fingers, but to admit to the fact that learning computer science through lectures and mathematical formulae was insufficient for me.

Not to mention that they made me feel like a giant ball of failure.

Despite the rigorous mathematical training I had received in high school, I had the hardest time making sense of the abstract concepts discussed in computer science and learning how to program.

But then,
during the second semester of my junior year, I got
a chance to take a class called "Computer Architecture,"
which I followed up with another class called "Operating
System (OS) Design and Implementation."

And little did I know,
that these two classes would radically change
my understanding of computer science

In my computer architecture class,
> we discussed what was inside a modern day computer. We learned how and why different hardware parts were designed, and also how they inter-operated with one another. When it came to assignments, we wrote programs that demonstrated our understanding of the behaviors and constraints of these hardware parts.

In my OS *design and implementation class,*
> we discussed the design principles behind a modern day operating system, and learned how it interacted with the available physical resources such as memory, processor, and hard disk storage units. To demonstrate our understanding of these ideas, we spent the semester programming a simple OS from the ground up.

And while taking these classes, I arrived at a profound moment of realization.

It turns out,
> the abstract programming concepts I was struggling with, **had a concrete physical base!**

As much as all the previous professors wanted to make computer science seem like a purely abstract discipline, I learned that many of the programming concepts were the way they were because of the physical constraints they had to deal with.

_{No wonder I couldn't understand what a "pointer" was.}

And with this realization,
the abstract concepts that I've been having such difficult time understanding, started to make a lot of sense.

You may be tempted to brush this off as a story of another youngster who had to go through long hard training before he could learn his lessons.

Unfortunately,
that is not the case here.

What took me three years to realize, was nothing more than the fact that computers are physical things. That they also abide **by the laws of physics.** That programming is not merely an act of symbolic manipulation, but also an act of working with the physical constraints of the computer, such as memories, processors, and external storage units. That a more intimate knowledge of hardware can help you understand the abstract paradigms found in programming languages.

<small>This could have been addressed with a different curriculum, no?</small>

But just to be clear,
I am not here to push for an overhaul in the undergraduate computer science curriculum. If this were merely an issue with university computer science curricula, I would not be so concerned. What troubles me is that the experience is far worse for those who do not study computer science.

How many people,
who have not studied computer science,
know
why
software crashes,
why
we all of a sudden run out of hard drive space,
why
the computer just gets slower and slower, or
why
we have to buy software just to read a document?
None that I know.

And yet,
they fall victim to these events day in and day out.
And what happens when they do? They feel
frustrated and powerless.
Why?
Because they do not understand what is actually going on.
Because they do not know how to respond, let alone prevent
it from happening in the future.

As a result, they often blame themselves for doing
something wrong or proceed to purchase the latest
and greatest in computer hardware, hoping the
problems will somehow go away.

Which, of course, they never do.

The profundity of this phenomenon becomes even
more alarming once you realize that this is not an
issue uniquely tied to hardware.

Have you ever asked a designer to explain how you can
trim a piece of digital photograph?

If you don't know any designers, just search Google.

If you do, they will invariably start walking you through
a series of actions that involve opening an application
such as Adobe Photoshop, then moving your mouse to
find and locate a button or a menu item to click.

But at the end of their demonstration, what would you have learned about the meaning of "trimming" in the digital domain? Besides the ability to mimic their actions, what would you have learned?

Nothing.

If one day Adobe decided to move the menu item to a different location, and rename their labels, this knowledge would become useless in that new context.

This is like getting a demonstration of how to cut a piece of paper with a pair of scissors, without ever learning about the fragility of paper. Without ever learning that the use of force against such fragility can give meaning to such verbs as "to trim." That you can do the same using a knife, a ruler, or perhaps an infinite number of other tools.

<small>If push comes to shove, you can always use your hands.</small>

Some people think this is because computers are inherently complex. They believe there is no way to reduce this complexity.

That would be true, if you believe that complexity is merely an attribute of the computer.

On the other hand, this is only partially true if you consider the fact that any complex physical phenomena can be understood more simply, once we understand the principles they are governed by.

<small>Otherwise, the discipline of science would go up in flames.</small>

Therefore, the perceived complexity of any artificial phenomena is partially a product

of design.

It is because the design does not help us understand the principles they are governed by. In fact, the general trend[1] in both computer science education and product design has been to hide instead of to reveal, to make abstract, instead of to make concrete.

---

[1] Researcher Matthew Crawford draws our attention to this phenomenon by citing the fact that vacuum cleaners no longer come with detailed schematics, and that some of the new Mercedes-Benz automobiles lack the dipstick, making it difficult for the owners to maintain the oil level themselves. (Crawford, 2010, 62.)

In an era where people demand to know where their
food
comes from, how their
tax dollars
are being spent, or how much
power
their appliances use, I find it ironic that we can stay calm about an invention that refuses to reveal its inner-workings while being so deeply integrated into our lives.

It seems only natural that we should demand that we have a way of knowing what is actually going on inside a computer. That we have a say in whether our software should risk not being responsive to our actions. That we be able to trim a digital photograph without depending on a software application like Photoshop.

_{Has anyone else wondered about this?}

Is this an issue of education and awareness?
Perhaps.
But framing it as such gives the impression that the solution is to merely teach everyone the ins and outs of computer hardware and software. Is this an issue of usability?
Perhaps.
But framing it as such gives the impression that the solution is to merely make computers easy to use. Is this an issue of making more software available free-of-charge?
Perhaps.
But framing it as such gives the impression that the solution is to merely have more software.

I think the issue is far more fundamental.
What we are dealing with here
is an abusive relationship.

The question most often asked about an abusive relationship is why the abused don't just leave the abuser.

Well, first of all,
they may be unaware. If they have never been in a healthy relationship, they may be lead to believe that their relationship is not abusive, but normal. In this case, it doesn't even occur to them that there's exists another option.

Second,
they may be afraid of the consequences. The promise of even greater violence, for instance, can feel ever so imminent, that leaving may not be considered an option.

Third,
they may be overwhelmed by a sense of shame. If they are led to believe that they themselves are to be blamed for the abuse, they will think they have no choice but to suffer, because no matter who they are with, the same result will arise.

Fourth,
they may be blinded by faith. There can exist a strong belief that the abuser will eventually change for the better, and that they have no choice, but to simply wait.

As you can see there are many reasons why the abused don't leave the abuser.

But the basic pattern is that the abused feels that leaving
is not an option.
That they don't feel they have the freedom to leave.

In the same way,
most of us
—largely unbeknownst to ourselves—
put up with the current incarnation of the personal computer, for the same reason that we think that we have no choice, but to accept it as it is.

Most of us are unaware of the fact that our
relationship to computers can be better, or
even simply different from the way it is now.

Most of us don't even feel that we have the freedom
not to use the computer.
Because we're worried about the negative repercussions.

And we blame
ourselves
for forgetting to save our documents,
and blindly believe
that the next version of our computers or software
applications will eventually come out to change
things for the better.

Simply put,
we do not feel empowered enough to feel
a sense of freedom
in our relationship to computer technology.

The kind of freedom that can get us to imagine
a new kind of relationship between man and machine.
The kind that can get us to imagine
leaving the relationship at will.
The kind that can help us
engage in a dialogue with the machine,
Instead of being forced to blame ourselves.
The kind that can help us
to proactively find solutions to our problems
Instead of passively awaiting for things
to change for the better.

At first,
I thought this was because "freedom" was not important
to the original designers of personal computers. But after
some quick research, I learned
that this was not the case.

Most modern concepts surrounding the idea of personal computing, turns out to be invented in the U.S. during the latter half of the 1960s, an era best known for its
hippie sucbulture,
a youth movement that valued
peace, love, and freedom.
These youths created a countercultural movement for liberation in society to promote this effort.

In *What the Dormouse Said,* journalist John Markoff tells the story of several prominent computer scientists.

Many of whom were hippies.

These were stories of scientists working in either university or corporate research labs from the 1950s through the 1970s who explored how to improve human intelligence, not only through computing, but also through psychedelic drugs such as LSD.

What was remarkable about these stories was that they were less about technology and more about the personal relationships of these scientists. The stories talked about their drug use, love of sex and rock and roll, as well as their engagements in political protests.

What these stories amounted to was a clear picture of what these researchers
—the ones who would eventually be credited as critical contributors to the invention of the modern day personal computers—
were after,
which was a vision.
A vision of computers serving people as tools for networking, community building, and peacemaking.[2]

[2] Many of those pioneering researchers were actively exploring the enhancement of human intelligence both through computing and through mind-altering drugs, spiritual inquiry, sexual experimentation, and other aspects of the political and social counter-culture. Many of the most critical contributions to what would eventually become the personal computer industry were made by people motivated not by money, but by a vision of the potential for computers to serve people as tools for networking, community building, and peacemaking. (Hasbrouck, 2005)

One such computer scientist was a person by the name of Dr. Douglas Engelbart, most well-known for giving a technology demonstration in 1968, amicably referred to as "The Mother of All Demos."

Often credited as the preliminary vision of personal computing, the demo showcased almost all of the concepts still present in the modern paradigm of personal computing: the mouse, hypertext, networked computers, and even the precursors to the Graphical User Interface.

And in his paper "Augmenting Human Intellect: A Conceptual Framework," he clearly talks about the importance of freedom being afforded by the design of computer systems if it wishes to help humanity solve the various and complex problems we face.

> As a leader, Engelbart was soft-spoken, but he was remarkably focused and sometimes even fiery about what he was trying to accomplish. His strength was that he saw things from the point of view of the user and then challenged his programmers to figure out how to make his ideas work as part of the overall design.
> **JOHN MARKOFF / JOURNALIST**

Another prominent figure was a software engineer named Richard Stallman, most well-known for starting what is called the
Free Software Movement.

> [Richard Stallman's best-known work is] called EMACS, which allowed users to limitlessly customize it—its wide-open architecture encouraged people to add to it, improve it endlessly. He distributed the program free to anyone who agreed to his one condition: "they give back all extensions they made, so as to help EMACS improve. I called this arrangement 'the EMACS commune,'" he wrote. "As I shared, it was their duty to share; to work with each other rather than against."
>
> STEVEN LEVY / JOURNALIST

In his article "What is Free Software?" Stallman says that a software program is considered free software if its users have the following freedoms:

1. *The freedom to run the program, for any purpose (freedom 0).*

2. *The freedom to study how the program works, and change it so it does your computing as you wish (freedom 1). Access to the source code is a precondition for this.*

3. *The freedom to redistribute copies so you can help your neighbor (freedom 2).*

4. *The freedom to distribute copies of your modified versions to others (freedom 3). By doing this you can give the whole community a chance to benefit from your changes. Access to the source code is a precondition for this.*

Needless to say, there were others as well. But what was clear was that the more research I did, the more it became clear that the kind of personal computing these pioneers had in mind
was not the same as the one we were experiencing now.

The ideas of peace, love, and freedom were deeply important to the people of their generation. And as far as I could tell, they wanted these values to be reflected in the idea of personal computing.

It was tremendously inspiring to learn of this.

But while I was inspired by their ideas,
I didn't fully understand them.

I felt that the idea of freedom had a much more concrete meaning to them than meets the eye.

Yet,
having never fully experienced the 1970s, let alone the 1960s, I wondered if I would ever be able to understand them enough to translate their ideas into action.

That is,

until I met a furniture maker
named Tucker Houlihan.

[3] At this point in my life, a mentor had suggested that I leave behind what I had, to do something different, something I wasn't good at, something I did not understand, to get a new perspective. In the beginning, I thought that meant going to get a Ph.D. in Computer Science. But through a chance encounter with a friend of a friend, I was made aware of the fact that a better choice would be to go to an art school, because that was most certainly doing something different, something I was not good at, something I did not understand.

I met Tucker for the first time while I was visiting the Rhode Island School of Design (RISD).[3]

At the time,
I was a potential applicant to their digital media program, and one of the students in the program thought that I should meet Tucker before I left.

When I asked this student who Tucker was, he explained that he was an instructor, an independent furniture maker, and the head of the graduate students' woodshop.

I was confused.

My interest was in the digital arts.
Why should I meet a furniture maker?

Yet, he persisted.
In fact, he was adamant that I meet him.
So I decided to give him the benefit of the doubt.

But when I walked into the woodshop
where Tucker worked, I was taken aback.

First of all, the shop was
incredibly dusty.
There was wood debris everywhere.

And on top of that,
it was very loud.

The entire space was reverberating with a constant
whirring sound of giant fans coupled with a sharp,
loud buzzing noise coming from the shop machines.

Having spent most of my adult life working
in a clean and quiet office, the environment
came as a shock.

"What am I doing here?"
I thought to myself.

Feeling uncomfortable, I rushed myself, in
search of Tucker.

Before long, I spotted a well-built man with receding gray hair, sitting in a small office next to the woodshop.

"Are you Tucker?"
I asked. Sure enough, it was him.

After a quick introduction, we went into his office and talked for several minutes about my aspirations for graduate school, and whether he thought RISD could fulfill them. Although there wasn't anything in particular that I found surprising about what he said, I did find him to be a rather patient and considerate person. Each answer he gave me communicated a great sense of care in his choice of words, and how he chose to frame his answers. It was a pleasure just being in conversation with him.

> Mr. Houlihan was the first one to offer his time and space for students' development. Students felt his enthusiasm and care and transcended it to other students. This idea of supporting, I find it to be the most fundamental core of RISD.
> YUKI KAWAE / GRADUATE STUDENT

As I listened to his considered answers to each and every one of my questions, I became more curious about his teachings. So, I eventually decided to ask him about it.

"What is the first thing you teach your students in the furniture making class?"
I asked, suspecting that he would say something related to ergonomics. Having been exposed to the ideals of human-centered design[4] throughout my career, I thought that would make the most sense.

But then he said something quite unexpected. He said that he teaches them about materiality.

"Materiality?"
I asked, wondering if RISD was still stuck in the traditional ways of thinking and human-centered design hadn't made its way into their curriculum.

[4] A type of design philosophy in which the needs, wants, and limitations of human beings are given priority consideration. The main difference from other product design philosophies is that human-centered design tries to optimize the designed product or service around how users can, want, or need to use the product, rather than forcing them to change their behavior to accommodate the product.

"What do you mean by materiality? You mean like wood?"
I asked incredulously.

"Yes, like wood,"
he responded as-a-matter-of-factly.

"Really? What is there to learn about wood?"
I asked him, surprised.

After raising one of his eyebrows in a curious
way, he quickly rose from his seat.

"Oh, I'll show you."
he exclaimed with excitement.

He then quickly guided me out of his office, into the shop,
and showed me over to the corner, where a pile of lumber
was standing against the wall.

"You see this wood?"
He asked me, pointing at a piece of lumber tall enough to
almost hit the high ceiling of the woodshop.

"Sure."

"What can you tell me about it?"
He asked.

"What can I tell you about the wood?"

"Yeah."

"Uh... not sure what to tell you. It's...
wood."

"You see, when I look at this wood, I see its entire history.
I can tell you how old it is, what kind of climate it grew
up in, what kind of seasons it went through, how much
rain those seasons had."

"Really? How?"
I interrupted, incredulous of his claims.

"By looking at these rings."
he said, pointing at the lines deeply ingrained in the lumber. "And it's not just about the history. How do you expect to make anything with wood, if you don't understand it well enough? The wood isn't going to do whatever you will it to. It's going to do what it wants to. All you can do is negotiate. Good luck making furniture without learning about materiality!"

I was
stunned
at his outpouring of passion. I had never met someone who was so passionate about something I considered so utterly insignificant.

Like a piece of wood.

But then,
I was reminded of something my mentor at work had once said. He had said
that physics is a luxury
that software designers do not have and, therefore, must carefully work to create.

Until now, I had understood that as an encouragement for designers to take their work seriously. To be rigorous about making sure that the behavior of onscreen objects were designed with consistency in mind. Because without such care, users would get confused.

But no,
that was merely the tip of the iceberg. What Tucker made me realize was that the very idea of materiality was absent in the computer. Or to be more precise, the computer was one giant material. But it was a material in the sense that space was a material.
Just as a space was occupied by atoms and molecules that have yet to form the right kind of pattern to give rise to discrete physical matter, the computer was occupied by bits and bytes that have yet to form the right kind of pattern to give rise to discrete computational matter.

In this sense, software programmers were like material scientists, carefully putting together the bits and bytes in just the right way to give rise to discrete computational matter.

Except, these computational matters are never made tangible or even accessible to others besides the programmers. The only thing most of us are given access to is the "user interface." Which means that most of us cannot learn about computational matters the way Tucker can learn about wood.

This is what my mentor was trying to get at, when he talked about the importance of physics in software design. He was saying that without making the physics And I mean "physics," not "objects." directly tangible to people, they would never be able to learn anything about the computer, beyond just pressing buttons and hoping for the best. This was not merely about good design. This was about exercising *our right to learn.*

> [Whatever] we may think of the curtailment of other civil rights, we should fight to the last ditch to keep open the right to learn, the right to have examined in our schools not only what we believe, but what we do not believe; not only what our leaders say, but what the leaders of other groups and nations, and the leaders of other centuries have said.
>
> **W.E.B. DU BOIS / SOCIOLOGIST**

But that was not all. What Tucker also made me realize was that freedom is not merely an individual attribute acquired through politics or the legal system, but rather an attribute that emerges in negotiation with others. That whether in relation to another human being, or to a piece of wood, the negotiation was a requirement. That to claim that we have the freedom to do it "ourselves," when talking about our ability to make a piece of furniture, was an illusion produced by trivializing the materiality of wood.

But to recognize this fully, was to
let go of my preconceived notions
of human-centricity in design.

Perhaps I couldn't help but put my own species at the
center of the design process, but it didn't have to be that
way. In fact, nothing had to be at the center. Or if you
wish, everything had to be at the center.
The point being,
the very idea of a permanent center was flawed.

I have been too comfortable with the feeling
of anthropocentricity to realize the possibility
that there exists an alternative
to the kind of design centered around
the maximization of human happiness.

In retrospect, all these years I thought the act of design,
and of making,
was merely a means to an end,
where the end was denoted by a happy user.

But no,
what Tucker had taught me was that a happy user
is but a small part of a much larger equation.

That the act of making
was not merely a means to an end, but rather a significant
endeavor in and of itself that helps us not only learn about
the world, but also
how we can negotiate
our relationship to it.

In retrospect,
this is also what I realized during
my studies in computer science.

The act of programming was not a matter of
commanding the computer to do our bidding.
It was a matter of negotiating with its physical
properties, to achieve something we could not
achieve alone.

But the question still remained.

How was I to translate these ideas into action?

By now I was desperately craving a new set of
design principles. One that can move us away from
the abusive nature of our current relationship
to computers, and toward the kind that craftsmen
have with physical materials.[5]

The kind of relationship built on a sense
of mutual respect. The kind that can
bring a sense of balance
into the relationship.

[5] An argument can be made that expert computer programmers well-versed in languages such as Assembly and C are already engaged in the kind of relationship that craftsmen can engage with the physical materials.

But unlike the time I learned about the pioneers of
computer science, this time it was clear what I had
to do to make progress.

[6] After meeting with Tucker, I decided against enrolling in the digital media program at RISD.

I had to immerse myself into an environment,
where I could learn
to become a craftsman.[6]

A person needs to go live in a foreign country before she
can fully understand the meaning of the country's native
language, or before she can effectively translate between
their language and her own. In the same way, without
such an experience, I could never fully understand
what it means to make things
with physical materials.

What you'll find across these pages are the fruits
of a four-year-long immersive and embodied
enquiry into what it means to make something.

And not only what it means, but also
how it works as a creative process, and
why it matters
to our lives

And while this project began with my desire to improve
the relationship between human beings and computers,
I hope you'll find it as fascinating as I do how the ideas
can be generally applied
to cross-disciplinary and cross-cultural human
relationships, and to the greater discipline of design
and education. ■

Our society's growing reliance on computer systems that
were initially intended to help people make analyses and
decisions, but which have long since both
surpassed the understanding of their users
and become indispensable to them,
is a very serious development.
JOSEPH WEIZENBAUM / COMPUTER SCIENTIST

SLIM I find it quite interesting that when I'm building things in the physical world, I'm constantly aware of how strong the structure is. By mere touch and application of pressure I can get an immediate sense of the integrity of the structure. What's the equivalent in the virtual world?

It took me five minutes to make a cropping tool using a ruler, pencil, and a piece of black paper. Why does this feel more difficult in the virtual world?

As I was making a paper sculpture out of smaller polygon modules, I realized that I had bought exactly so many pieces of paper, because I thought I knew exactly how many polygons I needed to make the final form. But in the physical world, there's no guarantee that each polygon I make will be of a sufficiently good quality for use.

I guess this is why the idea of quality management arose back in the days. If I make ten polygons, I may have to throw three of them away because I smeared glue on it, or they don't fit quite right. This is obvious in hindsight, but for some reason surprising.

3

October 1, 2008, 8:17 p.m.

October 3, 2008, 6:01 p.m.

October 7, 2008, 9:31 a.m.

INTRODUCTION

"All designers do is make stuff look pretty."

That's what I told my department adviser in college.

• I was 21,
and arrogant.

But after spending the next nine years working
at a design firm, I learned that what designers
actually did was help improve people's lives.

> If people are made safer, more comfortable, more eager
> to purchase, more efficient—or just plain happier—the
> designer has succeeded.
> **HENRY DREYFUSS / INDUSTRIAL DESIGNER**

Needless to say, it was beyond embarrassing
to realize how wrong I was.

How unaware I was of my own prejudices.

But even more embarrassing,
was to realize that this was part of a broader pattern.
A pattern, where I would trivialize another discipline
based on my own narrow understanding.

Because even after I was proven wrong about design,
I found myself picking another target to put down.

This time,
fine arts.

I thought,
"Okay, design... That's fine. I get it. It's noble and useful.
It's good stuff. But fine arts? Psha... Now, that's just
straight up useless
and self-indulgent."

But I spent four years at an art school,
studying both visual and performing arts.

I made objects using physical materials like paper, charcoal,
clay, plaster, metals, wood, gouache, glass, plastic, and light.
Then when I realized the significance of the human body as
a form of physical material, I also made performances using
my own body through acting and dancing.

And as I reflected upon these experiences through
writing, I once again realized how wrong I was.

How unaware I was of my own prejudices.

But I also realized something else.

I realized that the act of making was
—in essence—
a challenge to realize our empathy
in relation to others different from ourselves.

That other could be a fellow human being, or it
could be a character in a story, a piece of wood, or
even your own body. These are all "others" we
often assume to know, but in reality,
do not.

I realized that at each and every moment of our lives,
when we are faced with someone or something that
we do not possess full awareness or comprehension
of, something that we cannot meaningfully connect
to, something that makes us feel uncomfortable,
there arises in that moment,
a potential for us to realize our empathy
through an empathic conversation.

And whether
—or to what degree—
that potential is realized becomes contingent
upon the dynamics of the relationships among:

The attitudes of the participants in the conversation.   1

The language used for the conversation   2

The space in which the conversation takes place.   3

In this book,
>we'll explore the necessary and sufficient conditions
>that must be present in this triadic relationship,
>before it can give rise
to an empathic conversation.

>Through the use of diagrams, essays, personal stories, and conversations, as well as animated shorts, installations, physical models, performances, and video sketches, I have explored and modeled the phenomena of empathic conversation, not merely to hypothesize how it works, but also to empower ourselves to devise better courses of action aimed at being more deliberate, effective, and efficient in the engagement, sustenance, and facilitation of such conversations.

If there is anything I have learned in the years of
working in the high-tech industry, it is that we
are slowly but surely moving into an era where
we will be surrounded by billions,
if not trillions,
of interconnected computing devices.

> [There] are now more computers, in the form of micro-
> processors, manufactured each year than there are living
> people. As early as 2002, the semiconductor industry touted
> that the world produces more transistors than grains of rice,
> and cheaper... Accurate production numbers are hard to
> come by, but a reasonable estimate is ten billion processors
> per year. And the number is growing rapidly.
> PETER LUCAS / FOUNDER OF MAYA DESIGN

Moreover,
just as the number of species on this planet has naturally
evolved to 8.7 million different varieties,[1] these computing devices will artificially evolve to take on an equally
mind-boggling variety of shapes and sizes, each designed
to serve a different purpose.

[1] The natural world contains about 8.7 million species, according to a new estimate described by scientists as the most accurate ever. (Black, 2011)

Just like how craftsmen have a different
tool for every occasion.

But that's not all.
Just as the natural ecosystem has empowered
us to make things that ultimately affect the
way we sustain and make meaning of our lives,
so will
this artificial ecosystem.

In fact,
it seems to want to take a step further by empowering
whomever
to more easily make
whatever, wherever, whenever.

When a 3D printer can in theory be anywhere, anything can be produced anywhere. For a particular object the world no longer must rely on limited production chains, locations, and, importantly, regulations for certain objects... We will have the reality of a weapon system that can be printed out form your desk. Anywhere there is a computer, there is a weapon.

CODY WILSON / MEMBER OF DEFENSE DISTRIBUTED

If this is the case,
And there is no going back.
the question of "why"
—of ethics—
becomes paramount.

And by ethics, I don't mean the kind that preaches a moral and virtuous life, but rather the kind that embraces the imperfections of humanity, and the vulnerabilities that stem from our inter-dependencies.

The kind of ethics that
As philosopher Emmanuel Levinas might say...
embody the wisdom of love
rather than the love of wisdom.

And that kind of ethics
cannot be complete
without empathy. ■

Somewhere around every seven years make a significant, if not complete, shift in your field. Thus, I shifted from numerical analysis, to hardware, to software, and so on, periodically, because you tend to use up your ideas. When you go to a new field, you have to start over as a baby. **You are no longer the big muckety muck** and you can start back there and you can start planting those acorns which will become the giant oaks.

RICHARD HAMMING / MATHEMATICIAN

SLIM It has finally become clear to me that after spending countless hours doing observational sculpting. 2D is a subjective way of looking at something. It is a fragile moment in time that vanishes with the slightest of movement. "Perspective" is a metaphor for one of the limitations of our minds.

Man-made design can become fashion. It can be trendy, cool, hip, etc... But natural beauty never goes out of style. Why? Or can it also? And why didn't this occur to me before?

Objects don't seem to exist by themselves.
They are always in the presence of space.

Objects are tangible. It is visible. It is what is drawn.
Space is intangible. It is invisible. It is what is not drawn.

Space is the relationship between objects, and a crucial part of the context that gives object meaning. Without space, objects are merely a subject of lust. It is space that gives objects the opportunity to enrich our interaction with the world.

October 30, 2008, 8:47 p.m.

October 30, 2008 8:49 p.m.

November 11, 2008 11:53 p.m.

PROLOGUE

About 10 years ago,

I had an incident with a friend, who was bipolar.[1]

> She was generally outgoing, optimistic, and cheerful. But from time to time, she would suddenly become depressed, pessimistic, and sometimes even suicidal.
>
> *I really wanted to help her.*
>
> I had always prided myself as a problem-solver, and I didn't see why I couldn't solve this problem. I felt it was the least I could do for her, as a friend.

So I started out by browsing websites, then
reading books, until I eventually found myself
at a local support group, looking for advice.

There,
I met a psychiatrist, who told me
that the most I could do as a friend
_{Besides encouraging her to seek professional help.}
was to try and empathize with her.

I was told that if she became depressed again, I should sit down with her and listen to her closely. Then when I felt I had a good understanding of how she was feeling and why, I should express that understanding back to her. And if my understanding turned out to be correct, she would feel understood, and that should be enough to make her feel better.

[1] Bipolar disorder, formerly called manic depression or manic-depressive illness, mental disorder characterized by recurrent depression or mania with abrupt or gradual onsets and recoveries. A bipolar person in the depressive phase may be sad, despondent, listless, lacking in energy, and unable to show interest in his or her surroundings or to enjoy him-self or herself and may have a poor appetite and disturbed sleep. The depressive state can be agitated—in which case sustained tension, over-activity, despair, and apprehensive delusions predominate—or it can be retarded—in which case the person's activity is slowed and reduced, the person is sad and dejected, and he or she suffers from self-depreciatory and self-condemnatory tendencies. (Encyclopædia Britannica Online.)

It sounded remarkably simple.

That is,

until I tried it one day.

What I quickly learned was that empathizing
with her was a lot more difficult than I thought.

.

All I was listening to was my friend's
yelling,
screaming,
and bawling,
along with her saying,
"You don't understand."

Wrapped up in chaos and noise, all I could do
was guess how she was feeling and why,
hoping that I would eventually get it right.

But before long,
I had run out of ideas,
and was unable to figure out what it was
that I was missing.

PROLOGUE

But then,
      something occurred to me.

      And I began to suspect that maybe something
I had done earlier,
      was what caused her to feel the way she
      was feeling now.

      It occurred to me that it was possible that she was
      feeling the way she was, because of something
I did,
      or because of something
I said.

      So I told her that.

And like magic,
her screaming and yelling subsided, as she sat there
quietly sobbing.

What I realized at that moment, was that
everything I had been telling her up to that
point, had been framed in such a way
that it was all her fault.

And I had nothing to do with it.

I saw her
as a problem to be solved,
and myself as a gift from God,
sent down to solve her problem.

Actually, I even started off thinking
I already knew the answer.

It was really simple.
She just had to
calm down
and stop being so negative.

All I really had to do was convince
her to adopt this solution.

I thought,
if I can only
explain this to her logically,
if I could just convince her to adopt this
solution, she'd magically come to her
senses and snap out of her depression.

But, it turns out,
I had gotten it all wrong.

The solution to the problem wasn't a matter of selling
her on my ideas. It was coming to realize my own false
assumptions, my implicit role-playing, my unawareness
of my own dishonesty.

The problem wasn't her.
It was me.

It was me who was delusional. It was me who had to
snap out of it. It was me who was preventing myself
from being able to empathize with her.

And once I became aware of this, all
I had to do was muster up the courage
to express it honestly.

And with that, I ended up with a story
that was completely unexpected, yet so
simple,
so
obvious,
and so perfectly
logical.

Albeit only in hindsight.

A story I couldn't understand why I hadn't thought
of in the first place. One that made me think,
"No wonder she was feeling the way she was."
One that not only resonated with her, but also myself.

Then something even more surprising happened.

She thanked me.

If I had ever been a witness to
a genuine and visceral expression
of gratitude,
this was it.

I was stunned.

Never once, did I think that I could be thanked
for listening to someone
and reflecting back my understanding.

I will never forget
      that moment,
when those two simple words
      "thank you,"
made their way through her tears,
   in that barely audible voice. ▪

Through art alone are we able to emerge from ourselves, to know what another person sees of the universe which is not the same as our own and of which, without art, the landscapes would remain as unknown to us as those that may exist in the moon. **Thanks to art,** instead of seeing one world only, our own, we see that world multiply itself and we have at our disposal as many as there are original artists, worlds more different one from the other than those which revolve in infinite space, worlds which, centuries after the extinction of the fire from which their light first emanated, send us still each one its special radiance.

MARCEL PROUST / NOVELIST

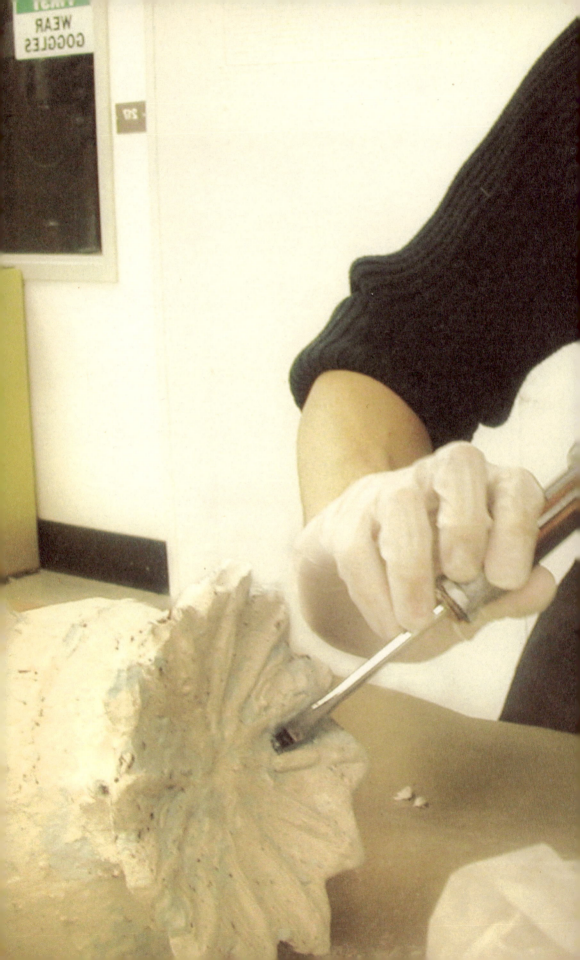

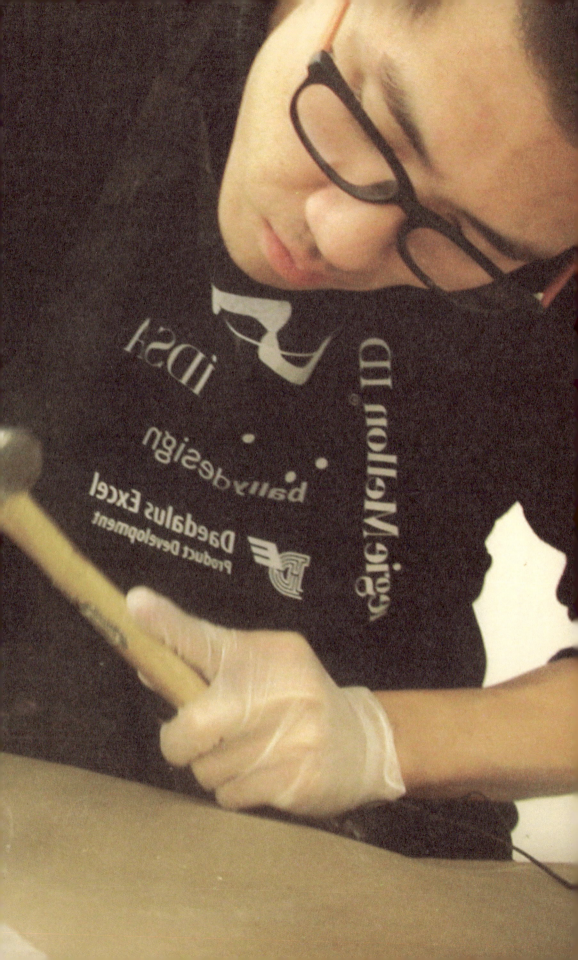

SLIM   Could you please introduce yourself, and talk briefly about your area of expertise?

I understand that your research deals with the process of learning and risk taking. Could you start by commenting on the relationship between learning and empathy?

What does that mean? That it begins with early attachments? Does that imply that they are not empathetic to begin with?

October 7, 2010, 10:00 a.m.

Yeah, I am Lewis P. Lipsitt,[1] professor emeritus of psychology, medical science, and human development at Brown University. I have been at Brown University since 1957, working in the field of child psychology development, particularly infant behavior and development.

DR. LIPSITT

[1] Founding director of Brown's Child Study Center from 1967 to 1991, Dr. Lipsitt was a visiting scientist at the NIMH in 1986–87, studying psychopathological risk-taking. At Brown University since 1957, he retired in July 1996 as a professor of psychology, medical science, and human development. Now an emeritus professor, he is also a research professor continuing longitudinal work into adulthood on 4,000 Rhode Island babies he and colleagues began studying in 1959. In April 2012, he was honored at the meetings of the U.S. Children's Bureau with the American Humane Association's Vincent de Francis Award, "in recognition of his outstanding research, thoughtful leadership, and ongoing advocacy on behalf of our nation's children."

Sure. The concept and the phenomenon of empathy touches very closely upon one of the most important concepts in the field of child development, which is attachment.[2] Having to do with the ways in which children—beginning in infancy—become attached to other people. We know of this as affectionate, loving relationships, or concern for other people.

Being attached to other people means that the child often uses that person as a model for their own behavior. And when we say that the person has come to be empathetic in later years, we assume that it all began with early attachments.

[2] Central to attachment theory is an infants' need for a committed caregiving relationship with one or a few adult figures. In the 1980s, the theory was extended to adults as well. (Bretherton, 1992, 759–775) (Hazan and Shaver, 1987, 511–524)

Well, that's... a very interesting issue. There are some people who believe that some kids are born with a lack of empathy,

Hm...

Hm!

SLIM   Then how does one get attached? Does it require spending a lot of time with that person? I'm guessing there is more to it than that.

Hmm...

Oh, wow...

Does it have to be a complementary stimulus? If the child smiles, and I frown. Does that affect the attachment?

Hm...

Hah.

Hah.

So you're saying that the baby is actively expecting the other person to respond back with a smile?

Wow!

Hm... Wow...

So is this expectation innate?

Hm.

or the lack of ability to attach to other people. And there may be something to that. After all, just about everything we know about human development and behavior comes in varieties. That is to say that there is a whole spectrum of just about everything from height to weight to intelligence. So why not attachment potential as well?

At the same time, we believe that just about everybody, if given the appropriate training early in life, will become attached to someone else.

Well, it takes time to have an attachment, of course, but it's not time alone. It's what we might call quality time. That is to say that it has to do with reciprocating interactions between two or more people, where I say something, and you respond, and I respond to the way you've reacted to what I say.

You can see this very early on in infant-parent relationships, when they're face-to-face, and the ways in which each of them energizes and potentiates activities in the other. For example, the baby smiles, and evokes a smile from mother, and mother's smile presents the child with another stimulus, a changing stimulus, a whole world of stimulations, that the child can then imitate.

(Smiles slightly) It does. When there is not a synchrony between the baby and anybody who is going face-to-face with the child, the baby becomes unsettled, even angry. For example, there is a phenomenon called the still face, where the baby smiles at me, and instead of smiling back, I just look at the baby like this (makes a still face). And before long, the baby starts going like this (imitates a baby looking around) as if to say "What is going on there? You're not responding to me adequately!"

Yes. They're expecting reciprocation of some sort. It might not be an actual smile, but it might be a touch to the chest or the cheek. Parents behave in many different ways, not just facially, but in terms of their posture, and their presentation of various tactile stimulations to the child.

Yeah. That's a very difficult question. We don't know exactly where it begins. If you have in front of you, a newborn child one day of age, and you smile at the child, it's very unlikely the child is going to smile back. So it seems to be something that is potentiated and accrues over time with additional experience. But it's quite possible that babies have the capacity

Hah...

SLIM But, how do babies know how to do that?

Wow!

Hm.

Then how does this differ, or does it differ, when the relationship is between the baby and an inanimate object and not mother?

Hm...!

So there's no distinction in the baby's mind as to whether the response they are expecting is originating from a human being or not?

Ah...

Does that relate to learning how to do things like walking?

very early on to respond to particular facial expressions. The neuroscientists are now talking about mirror neurons,[3] where there is a capacity we have in the brain to imitate. Even without actually imitating, we are recording an imitative response internally, and we'll eventually turn it into a mirror or an imitative reaction.

DR. LIPSITT

(Smiles slightly) We don't know an awful lot about what babies "know how" to do. We do know from research in the past half-century that newborns actually do learn, and they learn from the first day of life. They can be conditioned, much like Pavlovian[4] animals, like dogs.

If you can elicit a reflex from a child and pair with it a neutral stimulus, like a tone, that reflex will then be elicited by the previously neutral tone.

By the same token, you can operantly[5] condition them such that when they engage in a particular behavior, and you pop a bottle in their mouths just as they engage in that behavior, they're more likely to do it again in the next minute or so. And the more they get rewarded for engaging in that behavior, the more and more they're likely to do it. So both classical Pavlovian and operant conditioning are possible in young children.

Uh...

Babies are well-known to behave toward inanimate objects as if they are animate. For example, although this (pulls a string attached to a brown toy bear, causing the bear to flap its arms and legs) is not animate, (notices me smiling and starring at the toy) even you are behaving toward it as a baby would. You smile, you look curious as if to encourage it to do it some more. (Chuckles)

It just so happens that humans as animate stimulations are more effective, but they will learn to and react to inanimate objects as if they were human.

Of great importance is the fact that babies come into the world with a whole lot of reflexes. That is to say that without learning, they can already do a number of things. They can blink their eyes. You can put a pencil in their palm, and they will hold the pencil for a while, and so on.

There is a wide variety of reflexes, including salivation to tastes on the tongue. These are reflexive behaviors on which

[3] A neuron that fires both when an animal acts as well as when the animal observes the same action performed by another. It was discovered during an experiment where the researchers found the neurons they were monitoring on a monkey would respond when it saw a person pick up a piece of food as well as when it picked up the food itself. (Rizzolatti, Craighero, 2004, 169–192.) (Di Pellegrino, Fadiga, Fogassi, Gallese, and Rizzolatti, 1992, 91, 176-180)

[4] In a classical conditioning experiment, Russian physiologist Ivan P. Pavlov, placed a dog in a sound-shielded room. On each trial, the sound of a bell is promptly followed by food powder blown by an air puff into the dog's mouth. The tone of the bell is known as the conditioned stimulus, and the dog's salivation upon hearing this sound is the conditioned response. The strength of conditioning is measured in terms of the number of drops of saliva the dog secretes even when the food powder is omitted after the bell has rung. (Encyclopædia Britannica Online)

[5] American psychologist B.F. Skinner studied operant behavior through the use of rewards or punishment. For example, a hungry animal will respond to a situation in a way that is most natural for that animal. If one of these responses leads to the reward of food, it is likely that the specific response which led to the food reward will be repeated and thus learned. This also applies to an action that allows the animal to avoid painful or noxious stimuli. (Encyclopædia Britannica Online)

Hah.

Wow.

SLIM Then how about problem solving as opposed to walking? It seems like it there would be a difference since it is more abstract.

Hah!
Wow!

The baby seems highly self-aware. Would that be a fair statement? Maybe more so than adults?

I see. So you mean you can increase the self-awareness you have by exercising it? Will it degrade if you do not?

Wait a minute. Are you saying that even in their infancy, babies are actually communicating with themselves using some kind of a language of their own?

Really?

the world then capitalizes, so to speak. The environment capitalizes to develop more and more complicated behaviors from the child.

Just about everything begins as a neurally mediated reflex, and then the environment and experience take over and lodge upon the reflexes and enables the child to go far beyond the reflex. It just so happens that babies have a lot of reflexes that have to do with their arms and legs.

If you look at a very young baby you can see alternating movements in their legs. It's as if they're prepared to learn to walk. It's as if they've got the walking behavior in them, so to speak, already as a reflex. It just has to be nurtured and trained some more in order to make it happen at around eight months, ten months, one year of age.

Actually, problem solving is very much the same. Babies take stock of themselves and what they can reflexively do. Especially as they enlarge upon their behavioral repertoire, once they understand that (extending his arms), "Yes, my arm goes like this, and I see that I am in control of the way I'm moving my arm. Now if you move something across my visual field, I may capitalize on my ability to move my arm to grab it."

(Nodding) You could say that the baby is self-aware. But I wouldn't say more so than adults. Even self-awareness is a developmental phenomenon. It becomes more and more acute with increase in age and increase in experience.

I'm sure it increases with age. Especially with the development of language, the child comes to use language for communication not only with other people, but with one's self. You have seen children talking to themselves about what's going on, (imitating a baby looking around) if you have ever seen them say "Ka ka ka. Baw baw."

Yes.

Sure.

We, as adults talk to ourselves. We talk to ourselves about ourselves, about every action we might have had with a new person we've just met. That takes time and language to do. But there's every reason to believe that a child is—in

Hm...

Wow!

SLIM They're much more intelligent than I thought! So when they take stock, is this going inside their memory, and the next time they do this they expect the behavior will be the same?

Hah...

Hm...

Then at what point do they start differentiating these subtleties between the sound of mother's step vs. mother's friend's steps?

When I'm listening to you explain these ideas, it makes a lot of sense, but in the past, this was probably not at all obvious. How has the field of psychology changed during the time of your career?

Oh, wow...
Ha ha ha ha!

a way—communicating with himself even before he's got any language to comment to himself.

He's reacting to other people and taking stock—I guess that would be a good way of putting it—of what's going on around him, and how he's behaving toward it.

[Smiles and nods firmly]

Yes, they develop an appreciation very early in life that things are fairly orderly. For example, when they hear a certain footstep in the hallway, that's mother coming. And he is not surprised when mother comes afterwards. But if the mother's footsteps are heard coming down the stairs, and someone else shows up, the child will probably be surprised, because it's an unexpected event. Expectation of the regularities in the world are very important to children.

[Nods]

Yeah, they come to appreciate from very early on, those who are close to them, empathic to them, attached to them, and those others, the foreigners, that they have not experienced with much. That's how they develop the "I and thou" kind of relationship, I, you, and them. That becomes a very important distinction.

Yeah, it's been revolutionary. In the past half century, we've learned so much about babies.

I can tell you a little anecdote from my early days. I founded a laboratory—now called the Women and Infants Hospital—where nurses used to come in at our request with a baby. One time, I was testing the baby's visual capacities—we tested them for their vision, response to touch on the arms, that kind of thing—and I was passing a red cube in the babies' visual field, like this, (moves his hand across horizontally) and the nurse asked me, "What are you… What are you doing?" and I said, "I'm looking to find out whether this baby can see, and I'll know, if he follows the red cube across the visual field," and she said to me, "Oh, Dr. Lipsitt, don't you know babies cannot see in the first month of life?" and I said, "No, I didn't know. Watch this," (moves his hand across horizontally) and she was flabbergasted.

Hah.

Hah…

SLIM   Now that we know these things, it seems like it would have had a profound impact on how parents raise their children as well.

Can all this interaction ever get overwhelming? Could there be such a thing as too much interaction for the babies?

Ha ha ha!

Yeah, I was going to say that it sounds like babies are basically miniature versions of adults with simply fewer physical capabilities, but not much different at all. Is that a fair statement?

How does this relate to your research interests in risk-taking behavior?

I'm sorry, what is crib death?

She has worked with babies for over ten years, new-born babies, and had never observed this. Never been told. She was just dumbfounded when she saw the baby following the red cube not only horizontally, but also up and down.

That was the state of knowledge we were confronted with when we first started studying babies. Then we came along and said not only can they see, hear, and feel touch and pain, but they can also learn, (imitates the voice of a female nurse) "Oh, no! First day of life?" (returns to his own voice) "Yes, even on the first, second, third day of life. Some babies are better than others, but nonetheless newborns can learn." This was quite revolutionary at the time.

DR. LIPSITT

Of course mothers have always behaved closely with their children. But nowadays, people are more aware of what the babies are aware of, and all parents—fathers included—tend to interact much more with their babies than they have done in the past.

(Chuckles) There's research on this. If babies are stimulated to a large extent, let's say you keep presenting loud noise, like "boom, boom, boom," before you know it, the babies begin to frown, and eventually begin to cry, because it gets to be too much. They want to settle down and be quiet for a little while. Just like the rest of us.

(Nodding firmly)

Yes, that's a very fair statement. Yeah.

My interest in risk-taking behavior actually came from my observation of babies. I came to the conclusion rather early in my career that crib death.

It's called Sudden Infant Death Syndrome.[6] It's been a mystery. And it's still quite a mystery, but I've come to the hypothesis that there's a lot of behavior involved in the hazards associated with crib death. And that it's quite possible that between two and four months of age, when the baby stops becoming reflexive, and more cortically mediated in their behavior, more thoughtful so

[6] Sudden infant death syndrome (SIDS) is the unexpected, sudden death of a child under age one in which an autopsy does not show an explainable cause of death. (A.D.A.M. Medical Encyclopedia)

Hah.

Hm...

Oh, wow!

SLIM   So what exactly is happening during that transitional period? After a period of having reflexes, all of a sudden, I have to start using my brain to control myself?

So is it like using the reflex capacities as a training wheel to train the other side of the brain that is not about the reflexes?

So do babies miss a deadlines if they don't train up in that first few months of their lives when they reflexively explore their bodies and the environment?

to speak, it could be that during this transitional period, the babies that are vulnerable to crib death have failed to make the transition effectively. So their reflexes have not grown into cortically-mediated, learned, behaviors quickly enough to save their lives when they become entrapped and cannot breathe easily. So that got me very interested in risk-factors, what we call perinatal risk factors like prematurity or being born with the cord around their neck.

One time, I told an authority on infant behavior that it's possible that the behavior of the baby is implicated in the baby's own death. I told him that the baby might be getting himself in a compromising position in the crib with his face down on the mat, and doesn't know how to engage in the behavior that used to be reflexive, but now must be voluntary. And the man said, with a smile on his face (imitating an incredulous attitude), "Oh, come on now. Babies don't kill themselves." And I said, "Not only babies, but children kill themselves in many different ways by engaging in risky behaviors and having accidents.

Behavioral misadventures are essentially the biggest killer of children and youth adolescence. In fact, all the way up to age 22 or 24. Indeed, behavior is very much implicated in the death of children, and my hypothesis is that this is true even in newborns."

DR. LIPSITT

(Smiles) They have been using their brain all along, of course. But it was a more reflexive use of their brain. What you would call your old brain is what was controlling most of the behaviors up to two months of age. The "old brain" is what controls reflexive behavior. Those reflexes, their execution, provides babies with the opportunity to learn to do it themselves with the cortex.

Not the sides, but the top of the brain and the bottom of the brain. The old brain or subcortical brain, is at the bottom, and the cortical that is at the top is the cerebral cortex.[7]

[7] The cerebral cortex is a highly convoluted (wrinkled) outer layer of gray matter that the duplicate cerebral hemispheres is composed of the neurons of the cerebral cortex constitute the highest level of control in the hierarchy of the nervous system. Consequently, the terms "higher cerebral functions" and "higher cortical functions" are used by neurologists and neuroscientists to refer to all conscious mental activity, such as thinking, remembering, and reasoning, and to complex volitional behavior such as speaking and carrying out purposive movement. The terms also refer to the processing of information in the cerebral cortex, most of which takes place unconsciously. (Encyclopædia Britannica Online)

(Nods firmly) Yes, that's part of my supposition. Perhaps the babies born with some kind of neurological, neural deficit that inhibits or compromises the elicitation of the reflexes. And because these babies are reflexively weak, so to speak, they don't have as many opportunities as the neurotypical

SLIM So they could have gotten themselves in danger in the first two months as well.

And after the first two months that behavior will start to slow down.

Wow...

Do different children, based on early childhood experience, exhibit different kinds of attraction toward or aversion from risk?

Hm...

Hm...

What's driving them to do that? Are there evolutionary or other reasons for babies to take risks to be able to learn something even at a young age?

Hm...

Hm...

So do they know where to draw the line or is it also based on reflex?

child to self-administer those learning experiences that are going to turn the reflexes into deliberate learned behaviors.

(Nods) Right, they could have, but the reflex saves their lives during that period. Even though their reflexes are weaker, it's sufficient for the baby to be alarmed when their face is down on the mattress, and need to lift it off to breathe freely. But it may not be strong enough of a reflex to give himself a lot of trials to learn to do it voluntarily. Ninety-five percent of all babies who die of crib death die between two and four months of age. It's that window of risk and hazard there that does them in.

(Nods firmly) All reflexes including the grasp reflex become weaker and weaker over the first two months of life. It's as if nature intended to let them become taken over by some other mode of response.

Well, just as everything else, there are big individual differences in risk-taking propensities in young children and adults. Some like to drive very fast. Some like to get into fights. Some like to swim out farther than they should. As a consequence, the heavy-duty risk takers frequently take risks that can be fatal. That's why so many youths die of these so-called behavioral misadventures.

This is entirely speculative, but I think it's like a whole lot of other behaviors we engage in. Some things are not only good for us, but absolutely essential for us. Like eating. But it is possible to over-eat. There are people who have killed themselves over-eating and bloating themselves or becoming more and more obese, and dying young of obesity or other complications of obesity.

Some amount of risk-taking is there quite naturally in children, and they have to take some risks. Imagine a child getting up and walking for the first time. It rarely happens overnight. It's a gradual process, so you have to be willing as a child to take risks (imitates a child trying to stand up) to stand up, to fall over, to hurt yourself. But if you take too much of that kind of risk you get into trouble.

They draw the line according to their own defensive behaviors. If the child at the threshold of walking, falls

INTERVIEW

Oh...

SLIM You mean even the table has something to do with it?

So looking at risk as a bad thing is probably an over-generalization. There seem to be risks that are taken in order to acquire knowledge.

Hm...

Then do you think empathy has much to do with the learning experience that a child goes through in their early years?

Oh!

Then what if they have not had the experience of pain? Then you can't empathize with another person who experiences pain?

Then can one person's capacity to empathize fluctuate throughout their lives?

Hm...

Hm...

Ah...

To a specific person or in general?

down a lot, or falls down near a table and bumps his head frequently, he may stop standing up for a lot longer, before he feels safer.

Oh absolutely. A child can learn the very particular environment and see if the environment has hurt him before.

Some risk promotes behavior and some risk promotes intelligence. You have to go out on a limb cognitively in order to learn more, but excessive risk-taking could be hazardous.

I do. I think empathy is an out-growth of the earlier attachment process, and as the child relates closely to someone who is meaningful—who is there every day, who protects them from falling— as the child attaches to that person who is feeding him and holding him in a safe condition, the child will gradually develop empathy. If mother—when the child is five months of age—does something and goes "Ouch!" the child will frown and act like he's concerned about mother just having hurt herself, because by then he knows what it's like to get hurt.

(Thinks for a couple seconds, then smiles)

I guess I have to think about that for a while...

I think you can still empathize, but maybe not as profoundly. Even if you're deficient in pain perception, you might empathize with another person who is eating the same thing you are. As you taste something and feel the pleasure of sensation, you can appreciate that the other person is feeling the same thing, and that could be a kind of empathy.

Drawing now on clinical experience rather than research, a person can grow empathic with other people and endure some kind of a trauma in inter-personal relationships such that the sense of attachment goes away or diminishes, and may even turn into hostility. So we have human phenomena wherein people who used to love each other, now kill each other. That happens.

First, I would call attention to an individual, and as I think about it, I think it can become enlarged even more, like

SLIM So attachment is directly related to empathy and controls how much empathy you feel. And you can detach yourself by actively saying "Well, I'm not going to further empathize with that person."

Right, it's very conscious. It's not, "Oh, I don't know why I hate her," but rather, "I used to like that person, but I have decided that I am no longer going to like the person." It basically changes your perception.

One last question: What is different about the behavior of a child that is post-reflex, as in someone who has passed the first two months of life where the reflex was the primary influence on behavior?

Hm!

Wait, why is a new dog more complex than the previous one I liked?

Oh I see. So the abstracted idea of a dog is more complex than a dog?

one culture fighting another culture, that previously appreciated each other. People can change their minds—so to speak—about whom they identify with and whom they're going to attach to.

DR. LIPSITT

Yeah… This happens with adolescents all the time where you hear a young lady say, "She used to be my best friend, but now I hate her." (Smiles)

(Nods) Changes your future perception, yes.

Well, complexity is probably at the root of the answer to your question. There's an ever-growing complexity of behaviors that occur over time, so that we begin as being conditionable in the Pavlovian or the operant sense, and those conditioning processes evolve and become more elaborate so that as we come to like a certain dog, for example, it generalizes to other dogs we find.

When we find other dogs that are friendly toward us, the complexity of our relationship to the world increases with time. That, in a way, is a very good definition of maturity. That we come to appreciate nuances and complexities, and elaborations of things that we used to appreciate.

Oh, because it's a generalization from one dog to many dogs.

It is not just an abstraction, but also a more realistic extension of your reaction to the initial dog. Maybe a better example is our relationship to mother. Because once we're attached to mother, and learned all about reciprocating interactions that can occur between ourselves and another person, then we can generalize that kind of ability to attach and to empathize, to other people, so that we can come to love other people.

INTERVIEW

Hah...

Hmm...

SLIM   That sounds very Freudian.[8]

[8] At the time of this interview, I had a rather narrow and skewed understanding of Freudian psychology, primarily related to the Oedipus Complex. Since the interview, I have learned that some argue that Freud always recognized the importance of healthy attachment as an important variable in development, but that he was interested in infantile sexuality as a separate, but related, aspect of development. Some call for a re-evaluation of this endangered concept for the purpose of rediscovering that infantile sexuality with its emphasis on the body as the earliest means of emotional regulation and self-experience is the conduit to understanding our psychosomatic nature that is fundamental, along with related implications for development of gender, anxiety disorders, perversions, and other significant developmental and clinical variables. (Zamanian, 2011, 33–47)

You said the main difference between mature and less mature kids is this ability to generalize, but I'm still not sure how the ability to generalize relates to the idea of nuances.

Hah!

So then, the fact that you can first approach this person based on previous experience has allowed you to learn about the nuances in people?

Hm..

Oh, wow...

And, indeed, that's what most of us do. We grow up to become attached to somebody other than mother. And we often marry that person.

DR. LIPSITT

(Chuckles) Attachment is basic to Freudian psychology.

The relationship is this. If we relate to a certain woman, like our mother in certain ways, we can generalize from the pleasure of that relationship to another woman, to another woman, to another person, and to people who aren't quite like us, for example people from a different race.

So those generalizations are usually nuanced in the sense that they may start by you finding another person who has certain characteristics like your mother, and therefore you have an initial attachment to that person.

But nonetheless, that's a different person than your mother. So you may behave toward that person as you learned to behave toward mother, with respect, dutifully, and that sort of thing, but at the same time—honoring complexity—we develop other aspects of that relationship that are not like our relationship with mother.

It's partly a matter of categorical behavior, and what is sometimes called acquired distinctiveness.[9] A person that is like mother—the more experience you have with this person—becomes, in an acquired way, distinctive from mother in a way that is meaningful to you.

[9] Dr. Douglas Lawrence's classic demonstration shows that stimuli to which you learn to make a different response, become more distinctive, and stimuli to which you learn to make the same response, become more similar. The demonstration involved 20 animals trained on a successive discrimination to respond to a black and white stimulus and to ignore the curtains. Another 20 animals were trained to react to the presence or absence of the curtains and ignore the black and white stimulus. In a series of test situations, the animals tended to choose on the basis of the cue they had been taught to respond to; relearning was faster on the preferred than on the non-preferred cue; and the discrimination on the preferred cue was reversed more rapidly. It would seem that the learning of new instrumental responses is faster on a familiar cue than on a non-familiar one. The findings are interpreted in terms of the concept of the acquired distinctiveness of cues. (Lawrence, 1950, 175–188)

(Nods) Yes, that's a very good way of putting it.

In fact, that's something that is frequently capitalized upon in promoting race-relations.

If a child has grown up feeling negative, like a white child feeling negative toward a black child, he may not approach other black people so easily. So someone might engineer a situation in which that white child will have some experience with the black child and in the course of that

SLIM   That sheds a whole new light on shared interests.

Wow...

This has been fabulous! Thank you so much!

After I digest all this, would we be able to meet again?

experience, he is going to have the opportunity to like that person who he was averse to in the beginning.

Yes.

(Smiles) Much to talk about.

It's been a pleasure.

Sure.

DR. LIPSITT

When we talk about what's "true," we generally mean what is "real" as opposed to "imaginary..." But what is "the real"?
In the Cartesian scheme of things, reality is made of truths that exist a priori and are fixed and immutable. We discover truths but we don't create them. In the embodied philosophical frame, truth lies elsewhere. The new philosophers would argue **that if reality is something we make** together out of our shared experiences, then truths are not objective autonomous phenomena but, rather, the explanations we make about the common experiences that we share with each other. When we say "We seek the ultimate truth," we are really saying that we seek to know the full extent of how all of our relationships fit together in the grand scheme. Our pursuit of the truth is the search **for how we belong** to the larger picture and why.

JEREMY RIFKIN / ECONOMIST

SLIM

The process is mine.
All mine.
It is when the learning happens.
It is when you learn about the universe.
It is a verb.
I am a verb.

The product is yours.
All yours.
It is when I serve you.
It is what inspires your own process.
It is a noun.
You deserve it.

What I realized while planing wood is that maybe the most amazing standards system mankind has ever come up with is "flatness." Go around counting just how many man-made objects follow this standard.

November 23, 2008 2:50 p.m.

January 13, 2009, 9:05 p.m.

EMPATHY

It is an understatement to say

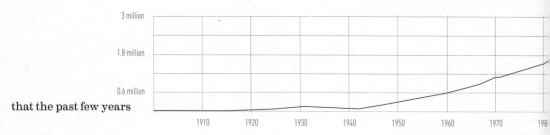

Yearly count of the English word "empathy" as it appears in 5.2 million books digitized by Google, Inc.

that the past few years

have seen a surge of interest surrounding empathy.

Numerous books and articles have been written about how anthropologists and evolutionary theorists have produced evidence that evolution is just as much about pro-social behavior and cooperation, as it is about physical violence and competition, accumulating an ever-growing amount of scientific evidence that we are a fundamentally empathic species.

> Humans have a tremendous capacity for resolving conflicts without violence. In today's world, we need to apply these skills in new ways and on a grander scale.
> DOUGLAS FRY / ANTHROPOLOGIST

And that's not all.

Modern brain scientists and child psychologists such as Frans De Waal, Michael Arbib, John Bowlby, and Mary Ainsworth have argued that human beings can be nurtured for sociability, attachment, affection, and companionship, leading to initiatives such as Ashoka to make a deliberate effort to bring empathy into education.

CHAPTER 1

And I worry about this.

Why?

Because it contradicts the prevailing belief that human beings are, by nature, prone to violence, aggression, and selfishness.

> If our extra-mundane observer were a knowledgeable ethologist, he would unavoidably draw the conclusion that man's social organization is very similar to that of rats, which are social and peaceful beings within their clans, but veritable devils toward all fellow members of their species not belonging to their own community.
>
> KONRAD LORENZ / ETHOLOGIST

[1] Many writers have advanced the notion that truth (or new ideas, or scientific theories) goes through a number of stages, starting with opposition and ending with acceptance. (Shallit, 2005, 3)

Whenever a shift starts to arise in the way we understand something fundamental to our belief system, such as the nature of human beings, it always seems to go through three stages of development:[1]

1   *It is attacked as absurd.*

2   *It is admitted as true, but obvious and insignificant.*

3   *It is seen to be so important that its adversaries claim that they themselves discovered it.*

I imagine we're somewhere between the first and second stage where there are many confusions, misunderstandings, and misrepresentations around what the fundamental shift entails.

What I worry is that these misunderstandings can make people label empathy as a mere "buzz word," without ever looking beyond its surface.

Take the fact that despite such large amounts of interest, there is not yet a consensus on the precise definition of empathy. So much so that in *These Things Called Empathy*, social psychologist Daniel Batson examines a whopping eight different ways people use the word.[2]

[2] The term empathy is currently applied to more than a half-dozen phenomena. These phenomena are related to one another, but they are not elements, aspects, facets, or components of a single thing that is empathy... Rather, each is a conceptually distinct, stand-alone psychological state. Further, each of these states has been called by names other than empathy. Opportunities for disagreement abound. (Batson, 2009, 3)

As a matter of fact, empathy is more often than not completely confused with another word, sympathy, which means "to feel sorry for someone." As a result, it is often misunderstood as a synonym for being nice, kind, polite, or even altruistic toward others.

And thus considered to be warm and fuzzy.

> There exists in fact no obligatory connection between empathy and kindness, and no animal can afford treating everyone nicely all the time.
> **FRANS DE WAAL / ETHOLOGIST**

And as if that's not enough, another popular misunderstanding is that empathy is a weakness. This is because people overload empathy with nothing but emotional contagion, which is an event where we become affected, and sometimes even overwhelmed, by other people's emotions.

It is misunderstandings like this that lead people to claim that the late Steve Jobs lacked empathy, because he was not always nice to people, and because he didn't go out and ask what people wanted before coming up with new product ideas.

Neither is proof of one's lack of empathy.

[3] Using this definition, when we say that someone "has empathy for x," we mean that they possess the necessary ability to realize their empathy in relation to x. And when we say that someone has "empathized with x" we mean that they have realized their empathy in relation to x.

What this leads me to believe is that if I wish to have a fighting chance at sharing with you what I mean by empathy, I have to at least provide an operational definition of the word up front. So here is, for the purpose of clarity, my operational definition[3] of empathy:

Empathy is an explanatory

Empathy is not one thing, it is a way to explain[4] a complex phenomena through an abstraction.

to experience an event, where we

From here on, let's call this event the "realization of empathy."

and/or understanding the expe-

An understanding[6] acquired without the realization of empathy will most likely be incomplete and/or inaccurate.

related meanings from the contex-

...principle for our potential... ...feel as if we are embodying... ...rience of an other, and its... ...and vantage point of that other.

[4] For further treatment on the idea of "explanatory principles," please refer to Gregory Bateson's essay "Metalogue: What is an Instinct?" (Bateson, 1972)

[5] Retaining the "as if" is not only less presumptuous than assuming you can "fully" embody or understand an other, but also more fruitful to retaining a healthy relationship between the self and an other without getting "lost in the other," which can be overwhelming.

Some use the word "capacity," which inaccurately frames a concept as nuanced as empathy as merely a container.

There is no way to prove that we are ever experiencing beyond the limits of "as if." [5]

Experience in the broadest sense: of feeling, thinking, and other changes to one's internal state and process.

A useful model for understanding what happens when you realize your empathy is to imagine the formation of symmetry between your experience with that of another with respect to a variety of axes, be it physical, mental, or emotional. The symmetry could be a static mapping in a point in time (metaphor) or a dynamic and imaginative mapping across time (simulation).

> The essence of metaphor is understanding and experiencing one kind of thing in terms of another.
> **GEORGE LAKOFF / COGNITIVE LINGUIST**

The more accurate and precise a mapping you can make with respect to as many different axes as possible, the greater resonance you will experience.

[6] In the past, understanding was criticized as being "purely intellectual." However, with the advent of the embodied mind theory, the separation between cognition and emotion, or more commonly known as the Cartesian mind-body separation, has become a heavily challenged idea in modern science. When someone criticizes an understanding to be "purely intellectual," or draws a distinction between understanding and comprehension, the problem often resides in the fact that the understanding was acquired without the realization of empathy, and thus inaccurate or incomplete. (Varela, 1991) (Lakoff, 1999)

The experience of such symmetry often affords the feeling that the other is an extension of ourselves; thus blurring the boundary between the self and the other. For this reason, a static notion of self and other is not as useful when talking about empathy.

A better model would be to put our conscious and subconscious processing of external stimuli at the center, then arrange the various sources of stimuli, according to how much you are aware of, can understand, and meaningfully connect to at any given moment.

One implication of this model is that much of what we traditionally consider as "self," can at times be an "other."

For example, if you cannot feel your foot, they'd be placed far away from the center.

> It makes sense to think of Yoga as a very thoroughly planned flow activity.
> MIHALY CSIKSZENTMIHALYI / PSYCHOLOGIST

On the other hand, if you're experiencing flow playing a musical instrument, that instrument would be placed very close to the center.

> [When in flow,] self-consciousness disappears, and the sense of time becomes distorted. An activity that produces such experiences is so gratifying that people are willing to do it for its own sake, with little concern for what they will get out of it, even when it is difficult, or dangerous.
> MIHALY CSIKSZENTMIHALYI / PSYCHOLOGIST

If there are times when you can't understand the thoughts you're having, those thoughts will be placed far from the center as well.

> Our thoughts, wishes, feelings, and fantasies cannot be seen, smelled, heard, or touched. They have no existence in physical space, and yet they are real, and we can observe them as they occur in time.
> HEINZ KOHUT / PSYCHOANALYST

self

In this model, an other is anyone or anything that we are not fully aware of, or cannot understand or meaningfully connect to at any given moment. Therefore, this allows what constitutes the self and the other to change across time, as sources of stimuli enter and exit a certain threshold of our own limitations of awareness, perception, and understanding.

Another implication of this model is that the word "other" does not mean "other people," and that we are capable of realizing our empathy in relation to non-human beings, even inanimate objects.[7]

This is not to anthropomorphize non-human beings, or to claim that they have minds like our own. It is to simply say that how we embody, imagine, understand, and ultimately connect with an other is not limited by their biological or neurological makeup, but rather how they are subjectively perceived.

> When the analyst's observations and interpretations are no longer viewed as "objective" facts, but as "subjective" organizations, the analytic field shifts immeasurably as the analyst is "dethroned" from the position of the "objective" observer, and becomes a co-participant in perceiving and constructing the analytic process.
> **JAMES FOSSHAGE / PSYCHOLOGIST**

By this token, the phrase "experience of an other" as used in this book and in the aforementioned operational definition of empathy is just as much about how the physical properties of raw materials change over time, as it is about how the emotions felt by a human being changes over time.

> Just as a writer surrenders to language, permitting the words to lead his hand across the page, so will stone, brick, wood, glass, and marble suggest to the architect the manner in which to use them. To denounce these correspondences between artists and material as mere animism would be to misunderstand. The architect who denies these connections does so at his own risk. The soul of his building will not be visible. He will have become a barbarian.
> **RICHARD SELZER / SURGEON**

---

[7] For those of you who have only heard the word empathy in relation to other human beings may find it interesting that the word "empathy" was originally no more than a translation of the German word "einfühlung" coined by 19th century German philosopher Robert Vischer to describe the human ability to feel "into" an art object. It wasn't until another German philosopher named Theodor Lipps came on the scene, that its use was expanded to also explain visual illusions as well as interpersonal understandings. It was this expanded use that influenced British psychologist Edward Titchener to coin the English translation. (Titchener, 1909). While I am well-aware of the criticisms made by the likes of Martin L. Hoffman on the technical differences between understanding people and understanding things, there are enough similarities for the purpose of this book for the broad definition to be useful. (Hoffman, 1981)

If your definitions or understanding of the aforementioned concepts conflict with mine, I simply invite you to take

> On the level of simple directions, commands, descriptions, the difficulty [of language] is not great. When the words mean "Look out!" "There is your food," "Go to the next white house and turn left," communication is clear. But when we hear words on the level of ideas and generalizations we cheer loudly, we grow angry, we storm the barricades—and often we do not know what the other man is saying.
>
> STUART CHASE / ECONOMIST

a moment to become aware of the conflict, and request that you kindly indulge me in the use of the operational definitions for the duration of reading this book, simply to minimize misunderstandings. ■

[Classically,] the word metaphor was defined as a novel or poetic linguistic expression where one or more words for a concept are used outside of its normal conventional meaning to express a similar concept. But such issues are not matters for definitions; they are empirical questions.

As a cognitive scientist and a linguist, one asks: What are the generalizations governing the linguistic expressions referred to classically as poetic metaphors? When this question is answered rigorously, the classical theory turns out to be false. The generalizations governing poetic metaphorical expressions are

not in language, but in thought:

They are general mappings across conceptual domains. Moreover, these general principles which take the form of conceptual mappings, apply not just to novel poetic expressions, but to much of ordinary everyday language. In short, the locus of metaphor is not in language at all, but in the way we conceptualize

one mental domain in terms of another.

GEORGE LAKOFF / COGNITIVE LINGUIST

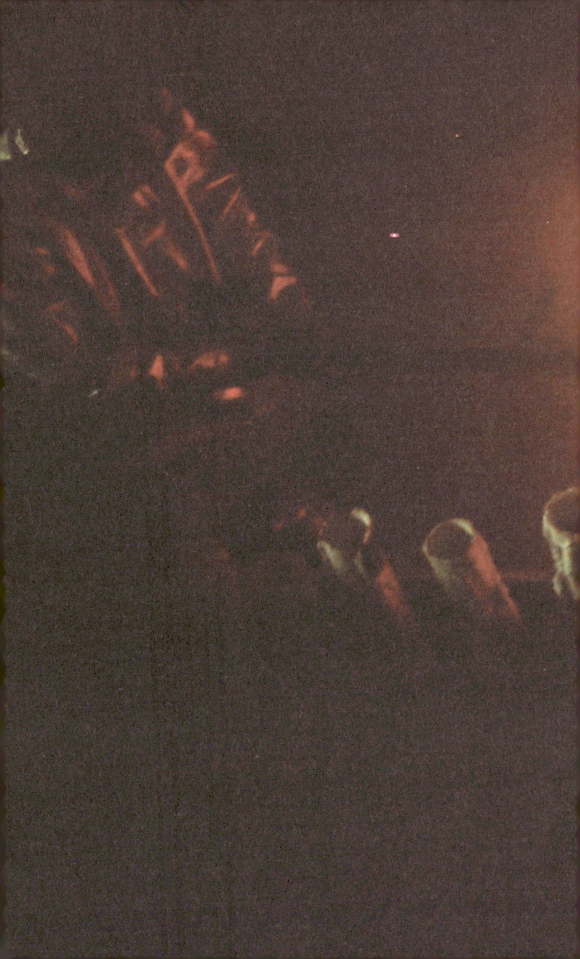

SLIM

A classmate said something quite profound the other day. We were to make a container of fruit out of a chunk of wood, and he said he went through a process where he first examined the piece of wood he was working with. Then he thought to himself that the chunk of wood was "too much material" to be made into a container of fruit. So he started to shave it off until he thought it had just enough material. That was enough of a jumping off point for him into design. No sketches, no ideas, nothing.

While this may seem like a simple statement, it has several layers of interesting aspects. First, he highlights the fact that in the physical world, one can visually recognize the resource being utilized. Second, since I am aware of the resource being used, I feel compelled to be efficient. Finally, the fact that such material use can lead us to make design decisions, or help us through a design process, is quite fascinating. Even if it is not about efficiency, the material is always reacting, which means you also have something to react or respond to. The beauty of physics at work.

I think I've always thought of the main function of "casting" as that of "duplicating," but there's actually a "translating" aspect that I now find more interesting. For example, you can translate a form from one material

89

January 30, 2009 2:50 a.m.

January 30, 2009 3:01 a.m.

to another through casting. This applies to both casting physical matter (i.e. metal) and in role casting (i.e. actors).

In class, I started by sculpting in plasticine, then cast it to plaster. When you go from one material to another it's not the "same" form, it is a "similar" form. The surface quality may be different, for example. So it retains some qualities, while losing others. This is often the very reason why one would cast from one material to another. For example, clay is easy to work with, and conducive to both additive and subtractive work. However, it can get damaged by the slightest poke, and it can't be painted. Plaster, on the other hand, is much more durable, and it can be painted. Bronze casting is also quite similar. One would pick a material such as clay that is easy to work with to make a form, cast it in wax, then use the lost wax technique[1] to make a mold that one can pour molten bronze into. The series of translations somehow reminds me of piping in UNIX.

Another aspect of casting across material is to get most of the work done in the material most conducive to getting work done, like clay, then to do the final detail work once it is cast in metal. In this sense, maybe compiling code is also a kind of casting?

In the physical world, making a tool is both simple and fundamental. During one of the metal casting sessions, our instructor told us that, as artists, making our own tools should be like second nature. Custom tools are usually a few minutes of fabrication away, and it can solve your specific problem much more cheaply and efficiently than any other general purpose tool that you may or may not have at your disposal at the time they are needed.

What's beautiful about the physical world is that one can just pick up some scrap materials like a piece of steel, and some left-over sheet metal to make the tools. This was once again, possible because we understood that "scrap" materials have specific physical properties, and that we have at our disposal "gluing" techniques and tools such as welding that allow us to combine these materials lying around that were meant for another purpose and make something wholly new from it.

---

[1] Lost-wax process, also called cire-perdue, is a method of metal casting in which a molten metal is poured into a mold that has been created by means of a wax model. Once the mold is made, the wax model is melted and drained away. A hollow core can be effected by the introduction of a heat-proof core that prevents the molten metal from totally filling the mold. (Encyclopædia Britannica Online)

January 30, 2009, 11:51 a.m.

REALIZING EMPATHY

Think of empathy as

a latent potential at one point in time,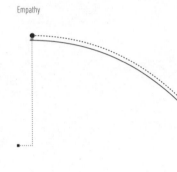

Empathy

Realized Empathy

⋯⋯▶ and its realization as an event occurring at another.

At times, you can get from the first point to the second instantaneously. This is a case when your empathy is provoked as an involuntary reflex, thus, empowering you to realize your empathy without much effort.

> [Empathy began] with the synchronization of bodies: running when others run, laughing when others laugh, crying when others cry, or yawning when others yawn.
> **FRANS DE WAAL / ETHOLOGIST**

CHAPTER 2

But at other times,
  empathy doesn't realize so easily.

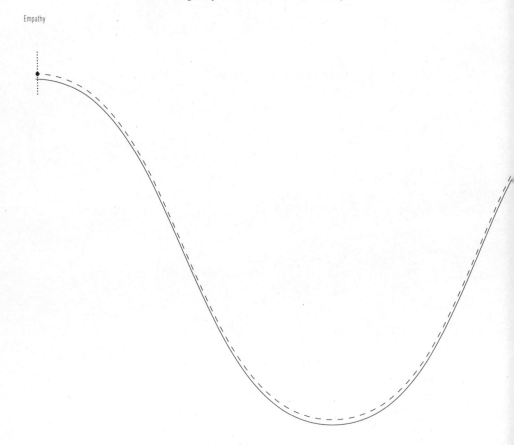

Think back to a time when you encountered an other
substantially different from what you were familiar
with, an other you had a difficult time understanding.
In relation to others like this, it is impossible to realize
your empathy without deliberate effort.

So naturally,
we may be led to ask ourselves why we should
bother to realize our empathy in relation to others
like that?

Why make the effort?

Wouldn't life be easier if we could just avoid
having to deal with such situations?

It would.

So why bother?

CHAPTER 2

[1] This is not to downplay the healing potential of realizing one's empathy in relation to another human being, but to simply draw attention to its less well-known aspects.

If you've asked this question before, you may be thinking that the benefits of realizing our empathy lie exclusively in helping other people feel better.[1]

> When we are feeling genuinely empathic, the other person usually experiences some degree of healing in our presence. Of course, we cannot "cure" the person on the spot through empathy, but empathy tends toward healing.
>
> PETER BREGGIN / PSYCHIATRIST

This is not the case.

Read the following out loud.

HI

Pause for a second, and say out loud what it means.

Seriously, put the book down and do this for me.

If you're like most people, you will have responded by saying that it means to casually greet someone.

Now then, whether you were part of that group or not, the question I have for you is this: Did it occur to you that it could mean the state of Hawaii?

Most people would say, "No."

Let's say that I walked up to you on the street, and read that same word out loud. Would it have occurred to you that I meant "High"?

Most people would say, "No."

When we hear a word, we tend to understand the meaning of that word by selecting from a pre-existing set of possible meanings. And how we narrow the selection down is determined by the context. We call this process "association." And this is not a reaction specific to words. It is applicable to our reaction to any stimuli.

> Associative thinking is the exercise of habit. It may be rigid or flexible, with a wide range of adaptability; yet it remains a habit in so far as it observes certain invariant rules of the game.
> **ARTHUR KOESTLER / NOVELIST**

For example, the same thing happens when you form first impressions of other people by sight alone. If the impression happens to be negative, we call it judgment.

But what fascinates me is that there exists another process through which these associations can be revised.

I say,
"Hi."

You say,
"Hello."

I say,
"No, I mean 'high,' as in up high."

You say,
"Oh."

A process known as
"conversation." [2]

[2] For a more in-depth and technical account of the process of conversation, you may be interested in the article "What is Conversation? How Can We Design for Effective Conversation?" by Hugh Dubberly and Paul Pangaro. (Dubberly, Pangaro, 2009)

To be clear,
    the kind of conversation I'm talking about doesn't
    require the exchange of spoken words. It just requires
    the exchange of stimuli.

    For example, you can think of what you're doing now,
    which is called "reading," as a conversation between
    you and me, taking place in your imagination, where
    the perception of the written words are the stimuli
    that helps simulate my presence, and voice your own
    opinions in response.

empathy   *sensitivity*   *perception*   *stimulus*   *signal*

But now,
    imagine for a moment, what would happen
    if we did not have access to such a process.

A world without conversations!
    All we would be doing is maintaining
    our regular routines and beliefs.

    This isn't to say that this is not a valuable endeavor. It
    is, because it helps regulate our sanity, and retain our
    sense of certainty. It's just that if all we do is maintain,
    we'd be stuck trying to fit everything into a pre-existing
    selection of possibilities, unable to learn anything new.

But the new can be jarring, even shocking.
It can also seem crazy and confusing.

> First, the self taken for granted till now is now made self-aware as the "familiar" by the other in the light of the self as familiar self, thereby learns the self "anew," deeper, in the light of the new-knowledge of the other, now the new familiar.
> **KUANG-MING WU / HERMENEUT**

As a matter of fact, chances are good that when you said "Oh," you were feeling uncomfortable, because you felt confused. After all, "No, I mean high as in up high" is not a response that makes sense to you in the given context.

> If it were, you'd have already made an association.

And what confuses things further is the fact that my saying such a thing implies that from my perspective it is, in fact, a meaningful response.

This is what we call a "paradox."

> Paradoxes can be fun... But paradoxes may be also disturbing; their study may reveal inadequacies, confusion, or incoherence in some of our most deeply entrenched principles and beliefs.
> **DORIS OLIN / PHILOSOPHER**

Paradox is a well-known harbinger of an uncomfortable feeling known as "dissonance."

Much like our general preference for harmony over cacophony, when faced with dissonance, we tend to work up an intense desire to find our way toward consonance.[3]

[3] Agreement of sounds; pleasing combination of sounds. The sounding together of two notes in harmony. (OED Online.)

> The existence of dissonance, being psychologically uncomfortable, will motivate the person to try to reduce the dissonance and achieve consonance. [In addition,] the person will actively avoid situations and information which would likely increase the dissonance.
> LEON FESTINGER / SOCIAL PSYCHOLOGIST

One of the ways we can achieve this is through labeling.[4]

For example, we can label the other "odd" or "weird." After all, wouldn't it make sense for a "weird" or "odd" person to say things that don't make any sense?

How's that for a logical argument?

[4] It may not be readily obvious, but disagreeing is also a form of labeling. Right before we disagree, we feel dissonance, and to achieve consonance we label the other "wrong," "ignorant," or maybe even "evil." For more on this topic, you may want to check out Kathryn Schulz's *Being Wrong*.

This is commonly known as "blaming."

> You know how blame is described in research? A way to discharge pain and discomfort.
> BRENÉ BROWN / SOCIAL RESEARCHER

What's another way to achieve consonance?

Let's say that the conversation is not between you and me, but between two friends, one man and one woman.

And he said,
 "That's interesting. Why did you say 'high as in up high'?"

And she said,
"Oh... Uh...

I'm... I'm sorry.

I just... didn't know what to say.

I haven't seen you in so long, and to bump into you like this was so unexpected.

The truth is, I've really missed you, and I just wanted to strike up a conversation.

But I felt awkward. So I thought maybe I should get you to laugh. I wanted to be funny. That's all.

But, of course, all I could think of was that stupid joke.

I'm sorry."

What just happened?

What happened is he tried to deliberately
realize his empathy by initiating
an "empathic conversation."

And as a result, he was able to better understand
her needs, motivations, thoughts, and feelings.

But that's not all,
he was also able to make a relationship between
two seemingly different and unrelated perspectives
—of hers and his—
This is a technique known as "bisociation,"

In contrast to "association."

and forms the very basis of creativity.

I have coined the term "bisociation" in order to make a distinction
between the routine skills of thinking on a single "plane," as it were,
and the creative act, which, as I shall try to show, always operates
on more than one plane.

AURTHUR KOESTLER / NOVELIST

A new understanding that comes from such
a product of bisociation is called an "insight."

When you acquire an insight, it changes your understanding, and develops your sensitivity by adding nuances to an other you thought you already knew. And in the process, it simultaneously brings about a feeling of both unexpectedness and obviousness by achieving a level of simplicity that makes you think, "Duh, of course she said that because she was feeling that way. Why else would she have said it?"

This kind of development process is known as "maturation."

[A very good definition of maturity is] that we come to
appreciate nuances, and complexities, and elaborations of
things that we used to appreciate.

LEWIS LIPSITT / DEVELOPMENTAL PSYCHOLOGIST

And through maturation, we can also acquire
a new choice of action in relation to the other
—a choice that you hadn't considered previously.

For example, he can now reflect
this insight back to her by saying,
"Oh, wow... I didn't realize you felt that way toward
me... You know what? I'm not doing anything tonight,
do you want to come over and catch up? I'll cook."

To which she could respond by saying,
"Oh, really? Yeah, I would love to.
Thanks for the invitation!"

As mundane as this may seem,

this is an example of "innovation."

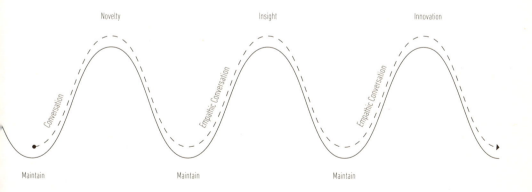

Some people think innovation requires
you to just make something wildly new.

No.

Innovation requires you to make something that
is not only new, but also meaningful in the context,
which it is being introduced to, enough to be
perceived as valuable.

For example, the dinner invitation was not only
a new idea that she did not expect, but it was also
meaningful and valuable to her.

What this means is that innovation is subjective.
What one person in one context finds innovative,
another person in another context may not.

A bushman may find the iPad novel, but not innovative.

In fact,
history is littered with amazing inventions that
stopped at being merely novel, because they failed
to be perceived as meaningful and valuable in the
context in which they were being introduced to.

We often say that they were "ahead of their time."

In other words, without realizing
empathy, innovation is impossible.

Not only that,
but when we present something that an other
considers innovative, she will also feel their
empathy realized.

Because of the unexpected nature of the innovation,
they will experience surprise, and because of the
meaningful nature, they will feel a sense of profound
resonance, of connection.

And when the amplitude of resonance is
sufficiently high, they may also become
overwhelmed with a sense of gratitude.

Remember the story in the Prologue?

One can say that if paradox is what precedes
an empathic conversation, surprise, resonance
and gratitude is what succeeds it.

And with this,
their understanding of the embodiment[5] of the innovation
will undergo a change. A change that can sometimes
fundamentally transform the nature and meaning of any
pre-existing relationships they may have with each other,
such that they become stronger and more meaningful.

[5] In this simple example, the innovation is an intangible verbalization of an idea. An idea that he would like to have her over for dinner, and cook for her. Thus, the embodiment of the innovation could be thought of as being himself, the presenter of the innovation. In other cases, the embodiment of the innovation may be a painting and its painter, or a product and its designer.

Needless to say, the sample exchange used here was a simplification. Engaging in an empathic conversation is rarely so smooth and painless. In fact, it can often be a long and arduous process.

Like the story I shared in the Prologue.

Whenever there is a self and one or more others in a situation where they must deliberately realize their empathy
in order to make something new,
—something neither of them could have made alone—
struggles are bound to be present. Whether the interaction is with a piece of raw material, a person, or even an idea, the same principles apply.

In fact,
any form of creative process, of making, be it painting, acting, composing, dancing, singing, choreographing, writing, sculpting, programming, or translating[6] can be framed as an empathic conversation.

And when they are framed in this fashion, the maker simply tries her best to realize their empathy in relation to the various others involved in the process, yet this gives rise to a plethora of side effects ranging from the acquisition of new knowledge, to creativity, insight, innovation, to maturation, connection, relational transformation, and beyond. And all these side effects feed into the general feeling of euphoria. A feeling powerful and addictive enough to convince the maker that the act of making is not merely about the product, but also about the process. ■

[6] People who do not speak multiple languages may find it odd that I put "translating" in there, but translating is a creative process that requires a great degree of empathy.

[In a] dialogue, when one person says something, the other person does not in general respond with exactly the same meaning as that seen by the first person. Rather, the meanings are only similar and not identical. Thus, when the second person replies, the first person sees a difference between what he meant to say and what the other person understood. On considering this difference, he may then be able to see something new, which is relevant both to his own views and to those of the other person. And so it can go back and forth, with **the continual emergence of a new content** that is common to both participants. Thus, in a dialogue, each person does not attempt to make common certain ideas or items of information that are already known to him. Rather, it may be said that the two people **are making something in common,** i.e., creating something new together.

DAVID BOHM / PHYSICIST

SLIM   When you are making in the physical world, you are able to see the results of your actions immediately. As a matter of fact, you can not only see, but also feel the result of your actions. For example, if you fold paper, you can not only see what kind of shadow it is making, but also how sturdy the fold is.

But here's the things. In the past I would have said that this was about "feedback." But no, I don't think that's quite right. The world is not "giving us feedback." It is being what it is, and when we act in relation to it, that being is sometimes expressed in a language that we can make meaning from. That's what we call "feedback." If the material is not being what it is, no matter what kind of "feedback" it gives, I cannot get to know it beyond a certain point. If I cannot get to know it beyond a certain point, then there's an artificial limit on what the relationship can grow to become.

March 1, 2009 3:02 p.m.

MAKING AND EMPATHY

A conversation is empathic, if and only if,

CHAPTER 3

it embodies the following four processes: Respecting   Listening

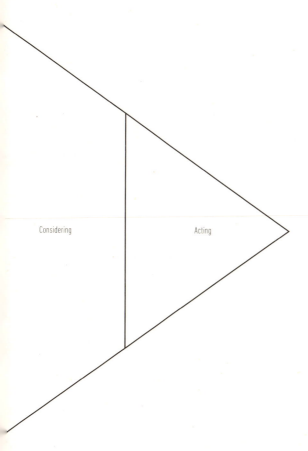

Ideally, they would also be carried out linearly.

But, of course,
this rarely happens in reality.

What is far more likely to happen,
   is that they will get all jumbled up like this:

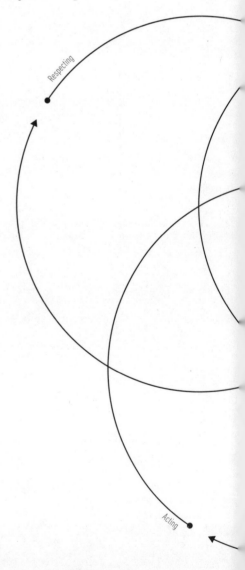

But let's talk about them one by one to get a better understanding of what each process entails.

What is
respecting?

Let me tell you a story...

"So what I did was…"

CHAPTER 3

I start to reminisce, standing in front of a white pedestal covered with glass objects.

        I hear my voice bounce around the
        wide open space of the art gallery.

        I feel the curious stares of my fellow students
        surrounding my peripheral vision.

VERB LIST COMPILATION:
ACTIONS TO RELATE TO
ONESELF (1967–1968)

RICHARD SERRA

to roll	to support	to join
to crease	to hook	to match
to fold	to suspend	to laminate
to store	to spread	to bond
to bend	to hang	to hinge
to shorten	to collect	to mark
to twist	of tension	to expand
to dapple	of gravity	to dilute
to crumple	of entropy	to light
to shave	of nature	to modulate
to tear	of grouping	to distill
to chip	of layering	of waves
to split	of felting	of electromagnetic
to cut	to grasp	of inertia
to sever	to tighten	of ionization
to drop	to bundle	of polarization
to remove	to heap	of refraction
to simplify	to gather	of tides
to differ	to scatter	of reflection
to disarrange	to arrange	of equilibrium
to open	to repair	of symmetry
to mix	to discard	of friction
to splash	to pair	to stretch
to knot	to distribute	to bounce
to spill	to surfeit	to erase
to droop	to complement	to spray
to flow	to enclose	to systematize
to curve	to surround	to refer
to lift	to encircle	to force
to inlay	to hole	of mapping
to impress	to cover	of location
to fire	to wrap	of context
to flood	to dig	of time
to smear	to tie	of carbonization
to rotate	to bind	to continue
to swirl	to weave	

[1] Richard Serra, (born Nov. 2, 1939, San Francisco, Calif., U.S.), American sculptor who is best known for his large-scale abstract steel sculptures, whose substantial presence forces viewers to engage with the physical qualities of the works and their particular sites. Like other minimalists of his generation, Serra steered clear of art as metaphor or symbol, proposing instead the idea of sculpture as a phenomenological experience of weight, gravity, space, process, and time. Yet his sculptures still evoke a sense of the sublime through their sheer scale and materiality. (Encyclopædia Britannica Online)

"...I read the words off of the Verb List by Richard Serra.[1] Then we acted them out on glass."
I exchange glances with my project partner.[2]
"What you see here is the result of acting out seven of the verbs,"
I explain as I point at each object.

[2] Alexandra Ben Abba / Artist

"To tear was the most interesting one,"
I say as I pick the last object up.

[3] Glass comes out of the furnace molten. Within minutes of entering room temperature, the liquid turns into a solid. In between those two states, glass can feel rather similar to a heavy lump of melted sugar going through a gradual change in viscosity. It is during this window of time, that most glass artists work with glass as material, and it is this dynamic nature of glass that makes glass both highly seductive and challenging to work with.

[4] Helen Lee / Artist and Designer

"We had to try all sorts of things before we got this one," I say as I try to hide how proud I was to have managed to tear a piece of glass.[3]
"It's not perfect, but it was interesting to learn that certain actions don't translate so well to glass."

"What do you mean, it doesn't translate so well?" The critic[4] asks.

"Well...
As you know, glass is very difficult to work with. It's very different from other materials," I say as if to show off my knowledge of glass.
"It acts like jelly when it's molten, which makes it very difficult to predict how it's going to behave. So what we had to do was wait until it cooled down to just the right temperature, cut it half way through, then pull them apart quickly. That was the only way to guarantee that the tear marks wouldn't heal themselves back up. Otherwise..."

"It sounds like
you were trying to make the glass look torn, as if it were a piece of paper,"
The critic interrupts.

"Oh, no, no, no!
We were trying to abstract the essence of what it means to tear, and translate it to glass," I interject in my defense.
But my conscience catches up to reveal its foolishness.

"Hm... Well, what you're doing is interesting. It's
a good start. But I think you need to be more respectful
of glass as a material,"
The critic remarks politely.

I nod, trying to refrain from feeling defensive.
"Al-right,
we have to move on. Whose
work are we going to see next?"
asks the critic, turning around to face the rest of the class.

As the class starts to trickle out of the space,
I stand still for a moment to gather my thoughts.

She was right.

I was being disrespectful.

I didn't think to see it that way
before, but, in essence, I was.

I had heard the word "to tear," matched it up with
one of the readily obvious meanings—one taken
from the context of working with paper—and force
it on glass. All the while ignoring the possibility that
the difference in material integrity can change the
context, and thus, change the meaning of the word.

And that's not all I had done.
I had also
blamed it
for being difficult, different, and unpredictable. Just
because it didn't behave the way I expected it to behave.
Just because it was not like the other materials I was
familiar with. Just because I lacked understanding.

[We] must recognize that what we have imagined about our
spouses, children, or co-workers is not factually true.
RICHARD SENNETT / SOCIOLOGIST

Standing alone in the empty space of the gallery, I start
to drown in my own embarrassment.

Not once
had I attempted to understand glass from the vantage
point of its uniqueness. Not once had I stopped comparing
it to other materials whose behaviors I found more
familiar and predictable. Not once had I thought of the
possibility that I was merely fishing for a reaction, one
that I considered a sign of a tear. Not once did I ponder
the simple fact that what makes a material glass will
—by definition—
live outside the frame of what makes a material paper.

How much more disrespectful could have I been?

We often confuse respecting with accommodating.

We think that by merely accommodating the differences we perceive of an other, we are, in fact, respecting them.

This is not the case.

Respecting requires us to accept the
fact that the other seems different,
because we expect them to be the same.

Just as we accept the fact that our body will have a difficult time accommodating a cold shower when it's expecting room temperature, we accept the fact that we'll have a difficult time accommodating an other that does not correspond to our expectations.

And as we accept this,
we also accept the possibility, that just as an impossible
shape is only impossible when viewed from a certain angle,
there exists an alternate angle from which to view the
other, where the difference will no longer seem significant.
An angle that can help us understand the difference
without contradicting or invalidating it. An angle that can
empower us to accept the other as they are.

And accepting this will be humbling.

Because we will not yet know
what the alternate angle is.

Yet the point of such admission is not to
feel ashamed of our lack of knowledge.

To the contrary,
it is to develop enough respect for the incomplete
and imperfect nature of our understanding.
Because it is only when we're able to do this, that
we will be open and motivated enough to find out
what it is that we do not know that we do not know.

CHAPTER 3

Now then.

What is
listening?

Let me tell you a story...

The sun is shining through

the floor-to-ceiling windows of the woodshop.

        I am standing across a tall piece of
        wood, clamped to the workbench.

        I hear mallets banging and clamps clanging,
    as I move my Japanese saw back and forth,
          along the top of the wood,
hoping to cut out a couple notches for joinery.

        I am in the zone, guiding the saw,
          shooting for a straight line,
until I notice an instructor[5]
        standing all the way across the room,
        staring at me in perfect stillness.

      "Yes?"
I look up, feeling self-conscious.

[5] Charles Appleton / Senior Critic / Rhode Island School of Design

"You know..."
The instructor responds, as I stand
upright to hear his next words.

"If you listen, the wood will tell you
how you're doing. It is very honest."
I stand staring, unsure of how to interpret
his Zen master-like comment.

"Do it again,"
the instructor suggests, as he starts to walk toward me.
"And this time, listen."

> [Listening] is a magnetic and strange thing, a creative force. Think how the friends that really listen to us are the ones we move toward, and we want to sit in their radius as though it did us good... When we are listened to, it creates us, makes us unfold and expand. Ideas actually begin to grow within us and come to life. You know how if a person laughs at your jokes you become funnier and funnier, and if he does not, every tiny little joke in you weakens up and dies.
>
> **BRENDA UELAND / WRITER**

I lean over and start to saw, as I take note of the
sound of the blade rubbing against the wood.
But I hear nothing of significance.

"Now..."
The instructor interrupts, as he reaches in,
unclamps the wood, lowers it, and clamps it
again. Less than two inches of the tall piece of
wood is now revealed above the workbench.

"Try again.
And listen carefully."

I reposition my saw,
and slowlystart to move it back and forth, quickly,
establishing a steady rhythm.

And then I hear it.

Or should I say
I don't hear it.

The rumbling noise, that is.

I guess it was a rumbling noise.
_{I am now thinking in hindsight.}

With the noise gone, all I am left with is what sounds like my teeth biting into an apple.

"Oh wow!
　I hear it now.
That's amazing!"
　I blurt out in awe in the absence of sound.

In retrospect,
　the moment he lowered the wood, I should have understood what I had done wrong.

I had clamped the wood too high, allowing it to vibrate, making a noise similar to that of a heavy piece of furniture being dragged across the floor.

The instructor was right.

The wood was being honest.

But until now,
I was not listening.
Or more precisely,
I heard the sound, but I was so busy trying
to get the wood to saw straight, that I didn't
try to understand what the sound meant.

Or worse yet,
I assumed I did,
because I thought the sound of sawing was,
Well...
the sound of sawing.

That if there could be any differences in
sound, that they were meaningless.

When in fact,
they were meaningless because I didn't
think they could be different.

> And because I didn't think they could be different,
> I didn't care enough to listen.

A present listener is cognitively, emotionally, and behaviorally attentive to the immediate context, and attuned to the people, place, and purpose within that context. Presence is a state of being: alert, attending to, and with the action, context, and matter at hand. A present listener is attuned to one's own and others' feelings, thoughts, and ideas. Situated in the immediate context, presence implies a willingness to be: with one's current state, the state of others, and the current actions and surroundings. Presence assumes knowledge and understanding to be cumulatively developed and constantly evolving, but being aware, as opposed to becoming aware, happens in the present moment.

LAURIE STAPLETON / EDUCATOR

> *And without listening,*
> I could perceive no differences,

A linguistic system is a series of differences of sound combined with a series of differences of ideas.

FERDINAND DE SAUSSURE / LINGUIST

> leaving behind an echo
> *of wasted honesty.*

We often confuse listening with hearing.

CHAPTER 3

We think that by merely perceiving the signals originating from the other, we are, in fact, listening to them.

This is not the case.

[6] From age 8 to 12, Glennie lost most of her hearing from nerve damage. She is profoundly deaf; that is, she hears some sounds, but the quality is extremely poor. In conversation, Glennie reads lips. In performance, she plays barefoot, and hears her own instrument and the orchestra by feeling vibrations through the floor and in her own body.

Listening requires that we make meaning from the signals we perceive from the other.

Perception is important, of course. After all, we cannot expect a person who is blind to be able to make meaning from visual signals alone, nor can we do so for someone overwhelmed with stimuli.

In fact, there exists a common misunderstanding that you cannot listen if you are deaf. This is simply not true. Listening is a whole body experience.

I suppose I don't hear things, but I listen, if you know what I mean. And there is a big difference between hearing and listening. So it's like a conversation, you know. When you speak to someone, it's one on one, and that's exactly how I play.
EVELYN GLENNIE[6] / PERCUSSIONIST

In order to listen to the other, we have to be sufficiently
present, so as to utilize enough of our senses to perceive
the variety of signals originating from the other.

> Because we have been trained since childhood not to
> listen while another is speaking, but rather to engage in the
> preparation of a defensive response in case it is needed, we
> have lost the child-like quality of listening with all of our sense
> organs: eyes, ears, touch, taste, and smell. Children until they
> are told that it is impolite, listen with all five of the senses plus
> one other: their own feelings.
> H.D. JOHNS / PSYCHOTHERAPIST

Just as it takes not only our ears,
but also our whole bodies
to listen to our favorite band in concert, it takes our
whole body and all its senses to listen to the other.

But once again,
even if the signals are perceptible, it is insufficient
if meaning cannot be made from them.

After all, we cannot expect someone born and
raised in one culture to be able to make meaning
from the language of another, just because the
words can be perceived.

But that's not all.
Even if we think we understand the meaning of
the signal, if the understanding is a result of mere
association, it may not be accurate or complete.

So just as a curious child verifies and develops their
understanding of the world by interacting with them,
we have to interact with the other[7] to verify and develop
the accuracy of our understanding of their signals.

[7] Some may wish to call this "asking questions." As a matter of fact, there is a common misconception that asking questions is about asking something of which you do not know, when in fact an equally valuable endeavor is to ask questions about what you think you know, but may not. To listen this way, you have to respect the other enough to be open to changing your understanding of the other through this process.

CHAPTER 3

And as we do this, we will start to become aware of
our own voices, the signals originating from within.
The kind that tells us that we're missing something, or that
there is something we don't fully understand.

These voices will be
    fleeting and fragile.
They will be easy to ignore
or to outright reject.

But if we're willing to listen to these signals just
as we are to the signals coming from the other,
they will alert us
to our own limits, our own biases and assumptions,
enough to reveal a more honest version of ourselves,
one with the ability to make the necessary bisociation
to better understand both the other and ourselves.

CHAPTER 3

Now then.

What is
considering?

Let me tell you a story...

I'm sitting at my desk.

Chair pulled in close. Back hunched forward. Fingers resting atop the touchpad of my Macbook Pro.

"Why did it take me this long to understand the meaning of these words?"
I ask myself, surprised and incredulous.
"What other words am I nodding to, without ever realizing that I do not understand them?"

For more than two months,
I have been trying to design a poster that illustrates nearly sixty typographic definitions, terms, and features.

Even with the poster measuring in at 20 by 30 inches, fitting them all in has been a challenge.
And as if that wasn't enough, the instructor[1] also told us to make the poster look not only organized, but also interesting.

Define and show an example of these 25 type terms.	Describe and show an example of these 29 parts of a letter form.		
		em space	vertex
		en space	light type
appropriate line length	apex	final	
appropriate text leading	arm	leg	lowercase
baseline	ascender	ligature	lowercase numerals
boldface type	barb	loop	median
cap height	beak	serif	old style figures
condensed type	bowl	shoulder	pica
dingbats	bracket	spine	point
extended type	counter	spur	roman type
inappropriate line length	cross bar	stem	small caps
inappropriate text italic type	cross stroke	stress	uppercase
leading	crotch	swash	uppercase numerals
	descenders	tail	x-height
	ear	terminal	

When asked how we could achieve such a thing,
he simply said that we must manage the hierarchy
by pulling some things into the foreground, while
pushing others into the background.

[1] Mark Laughlin / Senior Critic / Rhode Island School of Design

The idea sounded simple enough.
After all, what could be simpler
than pulling things forward and pushing things back?

As a matter of fact,
the idea of foreground and background was something
I had been introduced to several times in the past. It
had to do with coloring the images either black or
white to trick the eyes into confusing which image was
in the front, and which was in the back.

Yet,
even after two months of making revision after revision
after revision, I still hadn't been able to figure out how the
idea was supposed to help me organize large amounts of
information on a poster.

And I was left with a feeling
that I was still missing something.

But here I was,
    sitting in front of my computer,
bewildered and dumbfounded.

    Because just a few moments ago, I had
    accidentally stumbled upon a photograph
    of a diagonally standing wooden case.

    And as I stared deeply into the open
    space captured within its frame,
something clicked,
    and I was finally able to realize what I was missing.

    What I realized was that what he meant by foreground
    and background was not so much about pulling things to
    the front or pushing things to the back.

    What he meant was that it is possible to design a poster,
    such that the viewer
forgets that she is looking at a flat piece of paper.
    That when the contents come in to just the right
    relationship, there is a point at which the poster stops
    being a piece of paper, and, instead, becomes a metaphor
    of a fully three-dimensional space. A space where each
    typographic object can occupy its own rightful place.

The heart of the problem is not so much how we see objects in depth, as how we see the constant layout of the world around us. Space, as such, empty space, is not visible, but surfaces are.
WILLIAM J. GIBSON / PSYCHOLOGIST

    But until now,
        this was completely unclear. As a matter of fact, the
        words "foreground" and "background" did not even
        mean to me what they meant to him. The only way
        it could have, is if we both had a sufficiently similar
        experience that those same words pointed to.

"He should have said

'space'

Not 'foreground' and 'background,'"
I think to myself, squinting my eyes.

"If only he had chosen a different word, it wouldn't have taken me this long to understand what he meant!"
I try to blame the instructor, all the while realizing that hindsight is 20/20.

[2] About a year prior to this event, I attended the Basel Summer School of Design. There, designer Wolfgang Weingart used the word "air" to describe the space between letters, and he was correcting somebody using the word "space" to refer to the same thing. It occurs to me that he was also trying to explain the same idea as my instructor, and he felt "air" was a better word than "space."

It is unclear whether a different choice of words would have made a difference.[2] What is clear is that the experience of encountering this photograph has allowed me to relate those two words to an experience similar enough with the ones he had in mind. And as a result, I was finally able to understand him.

In fact,
now that I understood him, these were no longer just words.
They were metaphors.
Like a line of exquisite poetry, these two words were now capable of conjuring in my mind a visceral feeling of space.

It was as if I had felt, for the first time in my life, sufficiently lonely enough to realize that the word "lonely" did not mean "to feel unhappy due to the lack of company," but rather to feel as if a gust of air is passing through a large punctured wound in the stomach, bringing with it an outpouring of acid rupturing from within.

self   *shared experien*

Still awestruck, I started to ponder what I should do next.

But it doesn't take long.

I decide to scrap the design I had
been working on and start anew.

The instructor's meaning is now so clear and concrete in
my mind, that I start to have a vision. A vision of designing
a space atop the flat surface of the computer screen.

I can feel it guiding my hands to fill the canvas with
several pieces of typographic objects. And as I do,
I notice myself asking a question I did not ask before:

"Are these objects helping me
express the feeling of space?"
The answer is "no."

The feedback is
immediate, clear, and visceral.

I try moving some of them around, resizing
and rotating them, making them darker or
lighter, until the answer is "yes." Once again,
the feedback is immediate, clear, and visceral.

It is remarkable how much faster I am making progress,
yet how much more slowly I am making my decisions.

other

And as I repeat this process, I start to realize that
I'm asking another question I've not asked before.

"Will others feel
the same feeling of space that I feel,
when they look at this poster?"

Painting from nature is not copying the
object; it is realizing one's sensations.
PAUL CÉZANNE / PAINTER

It occurs to me that this is a question likely to be
asked by anyone wishing to capture a meaningful
experience so as to be able to share it with others.

I imagine for a moment the kind of care that great artists
must have put into making their work, into considering
each and every one of their moves, whether it be a brush
stroke, a dab of paint, a carving of clay, to try and share
that experience as clearly and as concretely as possible.

And as I do, I can't help but ask,
"What would happen if we put in the same kind
of consideration artists put into their work, to the
everyday exchange we engage in relation to others?"

We often confuse considering with thinking.

We think that by merely giving an other some thought, that, we are, in fact, considering them.

This is not the case.

Just as a chess master playing a world chess championship match cares about how effective and efficient her choices are in achieving her goals, considering requires
that we care enough
to want to choose an appropriate, effective, and efficient action sufficiently capable of sharing with an other a clear and concrete vision of the meaning we embody.

But as we consider the other, we have to also consider
our own abilities and constraints. After all, if the chosen
action is either infeasible or unsustainable, it cannot be
the most effective or efficient choice.

And it is also through such holistic considerations,
that we feel empowered enough to acquire
a sense of responsibility.

Because our goal is not to unilaterally
do things to the other,
but to purposefully respond, we care whether our actions
are indeed effective, and efficient in sharing with the other,
the meaning we embody.

So just as a snowboarder knows that her commitment to
continually adjusting her body
—in response to the changing terrains—
is directly related to how much ride time she can enjoy,
we commit to continually adjusting our understanding
of the other, because it is the only way to acquire a set
of action choices, proven to be effective, and efficient in
sharing with the other, the meaning we embody.

Now then.

What is
acting?

Let me tell you a story...

I am sitting in the dark,

quietly observing my peers. They are on stage, acting out a scene from *A Streetcar Named Desire*.[3]

The stage is packed with furniture, giving them barely enough space to move around. Stanley, the male lead, is aggressively going through the trunk belonging to Blanche, the female lead. Stanley is convinced that Blanche is lying about her intentions for returning home. Letters and clothes from Blanche's trunk lie scattered all over the floor, as she fights back, irritated.

"Good!"
A voice reverberates from the darkness. It is our director.[4]

"Let's explore this scene a little further."
She says.

I smile, quietly anticipating our director's next move. Having watched the correct rendition of the scene as enacted by Marlon Brando and Vivian Leigh, I am eager to learn how she'll direct the actors toward the right answer.

"How do you think Blanche is feeling in this scene?"
She asks my friend playing Blanche.

"Uh... Vulnerable?"
answers my friend.

"What else?"
asks the director.

"Mm... Defensive?"
she answers, reaching for another word.

"Have you ever been in the presence of a man who made you feel so vulnerable that you felt the need to defend yourself?"
asks the director.

My friend pauses. I can tell that she's surprised. After all, this is a first year acting class, and she is only 18-years old. What would she know about feeling vulnerable and defensive in front of man?

[3] A play in three acts by Tennessee Williams, first produced and published in 1947 and winner of the Pulitzer Prize for drama for that year. One of the most admired plays of its time, it concerns the mental and moral disintegration and ultimate ruin of Blanche DuBois, a former Southern belle. Her neurotic, genteel pretensions are no match for the harsh realities symbolized by her brutish brother-in-law, Stanley Kowalski. (Encyclopædia Britannica Online)

[4] Constance Crawford / Brown University / Adjunct Lecturer

My friend finally answers,
"... Yeah."

I squint my eyes, surprised to hear her answer.

"Can you remember the last time
you were in front of this man?"
continues the director.

"...Uh huh,"
she replies.

"See if you can remember what he
was wearing. Do you remember?"
the director asks, gently.

"Yeah..."
she says, softly.

"What was the color of his skin?"
the director asks, even more gently.

"White,"
she answers, with confidence.

"You don't have to answer out loud,"
says the director
"Just picture him in your head. Was he tall?
Was he looking down at you? What did he
smell like? Remember all the details."

The girl now looks visibly uncomfortable.
The director must have noticed.

"Stanley, go ahead and start going through her stuff."
Stanley starts to rummage through Blanche's
bag, as the director turns back to my friend.

"Now project that man you're afraid of onto Stanley.
Can you see him?
He is going through your stuff!"
Shouts the director, pointing at Stanley.

Next thing I know,

the studio goes silent, as Blanche turns to Stanley,

and begins to weep.

"That's it! Take that with you!"
The director exclaims.
"You can do it! Just say the lines!"
The director rushes in, as if to signify that the lines are meaningless.

Tears start running down Blanche's face, as her words fight their way through them. And as they do, each of them starts to land on my ears as if they're being physically delivered, one by one. They are strong, adamant, and confident, yet fragile, insecure, and vulnerable. It is profoundly different from the way it was acted a moment ago.

But that's not all.

It is also profoundly different from the way it was acted by Vivian Leigh.

CHAPTER 3

"Great!"
    yells out the director.

[5] Harold Bloom, an American writer, literary critic, and professor of the humanities at Yale University argues that Hamlet's "To be or not to be" is not a ponderance of suicide, but rather a reflection of "the growing inner-self, which he sometimes attempt to reject," (Bloom, 1998, 405) implying that the path to acting lies not in the act of merely mimicking the other, but rather in letting one's self "be" (Bloom, 1998, 422) one's self. He further contends that Shakespeare invented humanity, in that he prescribed the now-common practice of "over-hearing" ourselves, which drives our changes. (Bloom, 1998, 411)

    The scene ends.
The room erupts in applause.
    My hands are clapping, albeit numbed in paradox.

"How am I to understand this?"
I think to myself, confused.

"How am I to understand what just happened in front of my eyes?"

Coming into the acting class, I had assumed that acting was pretending to be someone you are not. And I thought directing was pointing someone toward an answer outside of themselves.

But what I just witnessed seems to be saying
that to act is to be in the moment, telling the story
of who we are.
It seems to be saying that to direct is to point in and
through the actors, such that they realize the lines spoken
and the names used are merely thin frames around their
own deeply nuanced and personal experiences.

> I read and heard the admonishments of fine performers again and again, that "You must lose yourself in the parts you play!" ... I [understood] that it was a warning to the vain and egocentric actors, but I had no idea how to [do] it... After many years of playing badly, I finally saw the light: I must find myself in the role!
>
> **UTA HAGEN / DRAMA TEACHER**

As a matter of fact,
the very discipline of theatre seems to be asking the world
"what does it mean to be who we are?"

> To be, or not to be, aye there's the point,
> To Die, to sleep, is that all? Aye all:
> No, to sleep, to dream, aye marry there it goes,
> For in that dream of death, when we awake,
> And borne before an everlasting Judge,
> From whence no passenger ever returned,
> The undiscovered country, at whose sight
> The happy smile, and the accursed damned.
> But for this, the joyful hope of this,
> Who'd bear the scorns and flattery of the world,
> Scorned by the right rich, the rich cursed of the poor?
> The widow being oppressed, the orphan wronged,
> The taste of hunger, or a tyrant's reign,
> And thousand more calamities besides,
> To grunt and sweat under this weary life,
> When that he may his full Quietus make,
> With a bare bodkin, who would this endure,
> But for a hope of something after death?
> Which puzzles the brain, and doth confound the sense,
> Which makes us rather bear those evils we have,
> Than fly to others that we know not of.
> Aye that, O this conscience makes cowards of us all,
> Lady in thy orisons, be all my sins remembered.
>
> **HAMLET / THE FIRST QUARTO OF HAMLET**

Because I have now realized that
each day, hour, minute, second,
we try to act,
as we struggle to find ourselves in different roles:
in one moment a son, in the next, a friend, an adult,
a parent, a professional, an employee.

And just as a novice actor struggles
as she mistakes acting for pretending
to be someone they are not,
at each moment in our lives we struggle
as we mistake playing roles
for being who we are.

As our minds try their best to keep us calm, to
keep us at the surface, to turn to stereotypes,
to seek and to retain certainty,
they construct false notions
of what it means to be good, kind, or even authentic,
from clichés and stereotypes we mistake for the real
meaning behind those words.

Our very desires to "be something," even if it's something
as benign as a good son or a good friend, often result in
nothing more than bad acting, and shallow entertainment,
leaving behind a sense of momentary pleasure, followed by
an immediate and intense feeling of emptiness.

But what is the alternative?
Without a clear definition of who we are or what is
entailed by our roles as sons, daughters, friends, parents,
leaders, and citizens, without a script or a series of
rehearsals for this play called life, what are we to do?

All the world is a stage.
And all the men and women,
merely players.
JAQUES / AS YOU LIKE IT

We often confuse acting with doing.

CHAPTER 3

We think that by merely doing something, that, we are, in fact, acting.

This is not the case.

To act, we have to let our being give rise to our doing. Just as our walking emerges from our desire to reach a destination, we have to let our doing emerge from the clarity of vision, of purpose, of action that arose from respecting, listening, and considering.

The foundation of acting is the reality of doing... Are you listening to me? Are you really listening to me? You're not pretending that you're listening; you're listening. You're really listening... That's the reality of doing.

SANFORD MEISNER / ACTING TEACHER

When this happens, we may find ourselves in silence
or in stillness, yet it will be meaningful. We may find
ourselves in service of another, yet it will be fulfilling.
We may find ourselves doing something we have
never done before, yet it will feel natural.

What happens when our doings emerge from a place
of such clarity is that we are able to embody
an honest expression
and channel it through our actions in a sincere manner.

Just as I was able to do in the Prologue.

And just as a piece of poetry written by a stranger
can realize and amplify the voice of the reader,
such sincere expression of honesty can realize
and amplify the voice of an other.

Just as it did with my friend in the Prologue.

Here are some simple ways to think about the
relationship between these four processes.

The first two
      are about opening you up to acquire a broader
      perspective. It is about being impressed and
      realizing your own empathy.

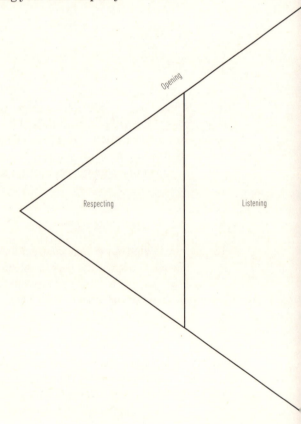

The latter two
are about focusing the broadened perspective
through a singular vision. It is about being
expressed and realizing an other's empathy.

Focusing

Considering   Acting

But once again, while it is convenient to talk
about these processes in such linear fashion,
the reality is never so straightforward.

Part of the reason why it is not so straightforward
is because an empathic conversation is essentially
a general way of learning something new
through lived experiences,
through embodiment.

In other words, the process of learning how to play
a new musical instrument has the same qualities
of engaging in an empathic conversation.

As you engage in an empathic conversation
with an other, you are not only developing the
necessary and sufficient sensitivity, knowledge,
and skill to realize your empathy in relation
to an other in the given context, but also
a general level of mastery
in your interaction with the other.

And until you acquire a sufficient amount of
sensitivity, knowledge, and skill, there will be
much frustration and many struggles.

Another part of the reason is that even when you do
have sufficient amounts of sensitivity, knowledge,
and skill, they themselves can be the very things that
prevent you from realizing your empathy.

> Culture is our shared assumed metaphor that stabilizes
> senseless chaos in to some sensible order, thereby pays
> a price—it tends to shut off other possibilities, alternative
> world-visions, and life-styles.
> KUANG-MING WU / HERMENEUT

In other words,
your way of interacting with the other can
become so habitual that it can become difficult
for you to interact with them in any other way.

Much of the empathy you realize in relation to them
will be automatic, their signals will mostly trigger you
to make instant associations, and anything out of the
ordinary may frustrate you, because it doesn't match your
long-developed expectations and knowledge of the other.

> Have you ever felt stuck while learning an instrument?

But as we discussed earlier,
in order to learn anything new about the other, we
have to be able to make bisociations. And in order to
make bisociations in relation to an other that you have
become extremely well acquainted with, you have to
partially or temporarily unlearn what you have learned.

Needless to say
this is a challenge.

So to help us overcome this challenge,
we have to employ a pair of attitudes
called humility and courage.

Now then.

What does it mean to employ
humility?

Let me tell you a story...

I am standing in the far corner

of the grimy metal shop. Public Enemy's "Fight the Power" is blasting
through the distorted PA system. The bass sound
is reverberating loudly alongside the whirls and
rumbles of the lathes, grinders, and Bridgeports.

In front of me,
are 20 rings, made of 1/8-inch brass
rods, waiting to be soldered.

I am excited at the opportunity to
solder for the first time in my life.

Earlier, I had already annealed the brass rods,
bent them around a mandrel, then trimmed and
forged them to the shape of rings. Soldering the
slightly open seams is the last step in the process.

I paste a little bit of flux in the seam,
and put a tiny ball of heated solder atop it.

I move the propane torch around the body of the ring, trying
my best to heat it up evenly. I stare curiously at the ring,
waiting for the solder to melt and flow in between the seam.

The torch hisses loudly.
The flux sizzles.

The brass glows orange.

I feel confident,
knowing that everything looks the same as it was
demonstrated by the instructor[6] earlier in the day.

[6] Peter Prip / Senior Critic / Rhode Island School of Design

"The solder should melt any moment now,"
I think to myself.

I make one trip around the ring. Then
another. And another. And another.

The moment never arrives.

I pause for a second not understanding what
is happening, and quickly inspect the ring.

I reignite the torch, and take it for another spin.
Then another. And another. And another.

As if that would change things.

The moment never arrives.

I am reminded of the saying that doing the same thing
over and over again, expecting different results, is the
very definition of insanity.

I stop.

"Is the flame not hot enough?"
I ask myself, all the while knowing that the flame
is of the same color the instructor wanted.

"Am I using the right solder?"
I wonder, as I retrieve the receipt for the
solder to double-check what I had bought.

I run through all the possibilities in my head
trying to figure out what could be the problem.

It's not the flux because I had already checked that a few
minutes ago. It couldn't be the ring because I forged it
in front of the instructor. If there was something wrong
with it, he would have said something.

"Whatever happened to materials being honest?"
I think to myself, frustrated.

It was a valid question, I thought. I was listening
to the sound of the torch, and looking for color
changes in the ring, and anything else I could think
of. I made sure all the materials I was using were
the right kinds. I considered everything. I was
doing my part, but the material was not.

In the midst of frustration, my waist bumps the
soldering station. Before I could do anything,
the solder rolls off the ring, falls to the ground,
and swiftly rolls under a nearby desk.

I pause to take a deep breath.

I put the torch down on the station and
reach for the propane tank to shut it off.

With one arm reaching for the cutting plier,
I pull a string of solder from the spool with
the other. I cut out a small piece of solder and
coat it with a dab of flux.

I turn the propane tank back on and relight
the torch with a flint. I point the torch at the
solder. The solder melts into a ball.

I turn the torch off, put it down, grab
a pair of tweezers and carefully transport the
small piece of solder to the top of the seam.
The tweezers slip.

The solder rolls off the tweezers, and my eyes follow
it to the edge of the station, where it falls to the
ground and rolls away until I can't see it anymore.

"Gahhhhhhhhhhh!"
I scream out loud.

It feels like I've been here forever.
I am tired, exhausted, and confused.

"Fuck metals,"
I think to myself.

I could finally understand why they call metals a "cold
material." It wasn't honest like wood. It was just harsh
and dead. After all, it was never alive the way a tree was.

A friend enters the shop.
"You okay?"
she asks.

I tell her about my frustration, and
she volunteers to take a look.

"Hm... That's interesting."
She remarks after giving it a go.

"What kind of brick is this?"
She asks, curiously.

"Brick? What brick?"
I respond, not knowing what to make of her question.

"This brick that your ring is on,"
she says as-a-matter-of-factly.

I pause for a moment in surprise, pondering
the meaning of this newfound association.

"I think the brick might be sucking up all the heat,
 which would explain why the solder wouldn't melt,"
she explains, as I continue to remain speechless.

"Here,"
she points to an unfamiliar pile of
bricks located next to the station.

"Let's try this one."
She reaches in for a different brick, replaces the
one I've been using, and takes another go at soldering.

In less than a second,
—like magic—
    the solder melts and starts to flow into the seam.

"Oh, duh.

That's... awesome.

Thank you so much!"
I exclaim, both embarrassed and excited.

She smiles, hands me the torch, and leaves.

As I marvel at the obviousness of
hindsight, I can't help but wonder how,
 —with no real visible indication—
I would have figured this out on my own.

Would it have occurred to me, if I had a more systematic
method or a set of tools for analysis?

No,

because knowing what kind of method or tools to use
would connote that I already knew more than I did.

Would it have occurred to me had I gone
through every single component in the setup?

No,

because that's what I thought I was already doing.

In fact,

I was oblivious that the brick was
even a component of the set up.

Even if I were meticulously going through every
arbitrary object in the mix, there's no saying
how long it would have taken before I exhausted
all the combinations to arrive at the brick.

Is this a limit that I simply cannot overcome?

We often confuse humility with modesty.

CHAPTER 3

We think that by being polite enough to be modest, or by underestimating ourselves, that we are, in fact, employing humility.

This is not the case.

To employ humility,
we have to trust that there's value
in respecting the incompleteness and
insufficiency of our own knowledge,
in doubting the things we know,
so as to consider how we can learn them anew.

What humility reminds us
is that our own opinion is the least interesting to learn,
because we already know them.

That we should raise the perceived value of
others' opinions, because we acknowledge our
default tendency to do the opposite.

That no matter how well we think we know the
other, there will always be a situation, in which our
knowledge will prove insufficient and incomplete.

Because the other
is always far more interesting and nuanced
than we can ever imagine them to be. And
because we can never be the sole authority
of truth and reality.

CHAPTER 3

Now then.

What does it mean to employ
courage?

Let me tell you a story...

It is eight o'clock in the morning.

I am sitting up high on a cold utility stool, leaning against a harsh metallic desk.

[7] RISD requires you draw bicycles as part of your undergraduate application. (Hovanesian, 2009)

Everything in the room looks gritty and industrial. There are small pieces of brown clay scattered all over the dusty floor. I am regretting the fact that I wore a light blue dress shirt, a pair of grey pleated trousers, and formal shoes.

I look around, nervous.

[8] Foundation Studies is the studio curriculum designed exclusively for first-year undergraduate students at RISD who have passed the rigorous application process. It is comprised of Drawing, Design, and Spatial Dynamics, each of which meets one full day per week. Freshmen are assigned to a section of approximately 20 students who attend the three studio classes together. (RISD, "Division of Foundation Studies")

There are around 20 freshmen students in the room, all of them 12 or more years younger than me. Rumor has it, they draw amazingly realistic bicycles.[7] I imagine their sketchbooks filled with beautiful drawings freshly rendered just moments before class. I ask myself if I am worthy of becoming a part of this prestigious freshmen foundation class.[8] Just a year ago, I didn't even know how to draw.
As a matter of fact,
I still don't.

The instructor[9] beckons us to the front of the classroom.
We quickly surround her as she begins her demonstration.

[9] Alba Corrado / Senior Critic / Rhode Island School of Design

With one quick motion, she shows us how to use a bone folder to make a clean and sharp crease on Bristol paper, and with another, she shows us how to fold along the crease, such that the paper folds cleanly.

"That's it?"
I think to myself, finding the demonstration trivial.

Just as I let my guard down, the instructor tells us to return to our seats, and to fold our own.

"Fold our own what?"
I wonder.

Anxiety strikes.
This was that art school creativity thing that I had been warned about.

I try to regain my confidence by reminding myself that I come with nine years of professional experience in the equally creative field of design. That over the years, I have amassed a number of methods that can help me be more creative.

I return to my desk, reassured. I reach inside my bag for a set of post-it notes. I start to brainstorm ideas around different forms I could fold. As I tell myself that there are no bad ideas, I sketch, sketch, and sketch some more in search of a design I like.

> I wrote the book *Design Methods*. What emerged in writing the book was that to use design methods one needs to be able to identify the right variables, the important ones, and to accept instability in the design problem itself. One has to transform the problem and the solution all in one mental act or process.
> **J. CHRISTOPHER JONES / DESIGNER**

A couple hours pass by, and I finally run out of ideas: none
of the ideas I have come up with thus far look promising.

Feeling anxious, I decide to skip lunch. I switch to another
method, hoping for a better result. The time keeps passing,
yet there's nary a hint of what I should fold.

It is now three o'clock in the afternoon.
    I am starving.

That nine years of experience I was counting on seems
almost too cruel for not extending a helping hand.

In a moment of desperation,
I decide to look around at what others are doing.

I notice a girl in the corner.[10] She seems intensely
focused on folding her paper. Even from afar, I can
see a large pile of folded objects atop her desk.

Curious of her vision, I leave my desk for hers.

As I get closer, I start to look more closely,

    but nothing catches my eyes.

I take another look.

Although the variety of objects is impressive,
there is none that seem particularly interesting.

    "This is it?"
I think to myself, disappointed.

    "Why does she look so confident and focused?"
I wonder, as I tap her on her shoulder.

---

[10] Chuan Liu / Architecture Student / Rhode Island School of Design

"Hey, what are you making?"
I ask, with a forced smile.

"I don't know,"
she answers. Her flippant answer echoes in my ears.

I   Don't   Know.

Just three simple words.

> It's a rather odd attitude for a scientist: wanting to know the answer before deciding what the questions are and how to answer them. It's more than odd: it's totally backwards, and in fact, antiscientific. If there is anything that characterizes the sciences at their best, it's the quality of not knowing where they can or should go, and then experimenting with ways to get there
>
> **MICHAEL FORTUN / HISTORIAN AND ANTHROPOLOGIST OF SCIENCE**

"What are these other ones?"
I ask again, unsure of what to make of her answer.

"I don't know... I'm just trying stuff out."
She responds.

"Really?"
I ask one last time, unconvinced.

"Yeah, really."
She responds, amused at my incredulity.

"That's a lie."
I think to myself.

If she doesn't know what she's doing, her hands cannot be moving. If she doesn't know, she cannot decide where to fold and in what direction. If she doesn't know, she cannot anticipate what kind of effect a fold could have on her subsequent folds. If she doesn't know, she could not have folded this many objects.

But then
it hits me like a ton of bricks.

This
is youth.
This
is what it means to have a beginner's mindset.
This is what it means to follow your heart, to trust yourself.

It is courage.

Never mind my lack of drawing skills.
Courage is what I lacked.

How cowardly was I to have come dressed to impress upon the students and the instructor that I am worthy of being allowed into the class? What did I think my resume, my previous title, or the way I dressed had to do with my creative abilities?

Perhaps much of my professional life was nothing more than hiding behind existing knowledge, formalized methods, and a fancy job title. Maybe all I had been, was a mere shadow of who I am, a bad imitation, at best, a closed minded, arrogant, dogmatic,
"adult"
stupefied by his own experience.

I have never, in my life,
felt like such a failure.

Perhaps an even greater challenge than achieving success, gaining recognition, or even to doing great work that blows people's minds, is to simply have the courage to not let anyone convince you that you're crazy.

Just because you do not know where you're headed, does not mean you're lost. Just because you cannot articulate your goals, it does not mean you don't have one.

But how are we to retain our identity in the midst of societal pressures abounding our lives? How are we to acquire a sense of direction and confidence without a clear vision of where we are headed? How are we to trust ourselves when we do not know who we are? How are we to muster the courage to face such insurmountable uncertainties?

Then...

it hits me, again.

What this girl means by "just trying stuff out" is not a naïve and undisciplined act of wandering. If that were the case, she could not have made so many different pieces of folded objects. What she means is that she is learning to trust the materials.

Just as a child learns how her actions affect others and why through exploration, she is doing the same with materials. Just as a child learns how to best respond to others and why through exploration, she is doing the same with materials. And just as this set of knowledge can help a child predict others' future actions and reactions, the same is happening between her and her materials.

And in this process, she is learning to develop a sense of trust in relation to her materials.

What the students are learning in this foundation class, is not merely how to make amazing pieces of folded objects.

They are discovering a source of trust
beyond themselves!

They are learning that the physical materials they are challenged to make with, is not only a source of uncertainty, but also a means to learn how best to respond to the very uncertainty it bears.

And through this experience, they are learning that the physical materials are not merely a means to execute their vision, but also a trustworthy partner that can both challenge and deepen their mastery of the material world at large.

That the fear and uncertainty, which emerges in our relationship to other materials is nothing but an indication that we have yet to empathize with them.

That the courage we need to muster in the face of such uncertainties, is not merely the courage to trust ourselves, but also
the materials.

We often confuse courage with naïve forms of risk-taking.

CHAPTER 3

We think that by being aggressive, we are, in fact, employing courage.

This is not the case.

To employ courage,
we have to trust that there's value
in listening to our fears.
in becoming honest with our vulnerabilities,
so as to test its validities and limits.

Just as our mothers used to walk a hundred meters just to make sure they had turned off the gas, we have to be prepared to do the things we find uncomfortable, so as to empower ourselves to resolve the source of that feeling of discomfort.

What courage reminds us
is that at any given moment in time, we have the option
to make our choice.

And by
making our choice,
I don't mean choosing from a pre-existing
set of habitual choices. I mean making new
choices that we have yet to make.

And by virtue of having never tried them,
choosing to make these choices will require that you take
a risk. Not only that, this new choice will often require
you not only trust yourself, but also the others involved,
which will add to the risk. But without making such new
choices, we will be unable to learn anything new. And
without learning something new, we will not be able to
fathom the full breadth of the choices that we have.

Now then.

What is the relationship
between courage and humility?

We often think humility and courage are opposites.

We think that humility is at one end of a line,

and courage on the other.

This is not the case.

Humility and courage

are points on a circle.
Most false dichotomies can be resolved by taking the
two points off of a line, and putting them on a circle.

As you travel along the circle, from humility
to courage, you will gain the sensitivity,
knowledge, and skill required for expression.

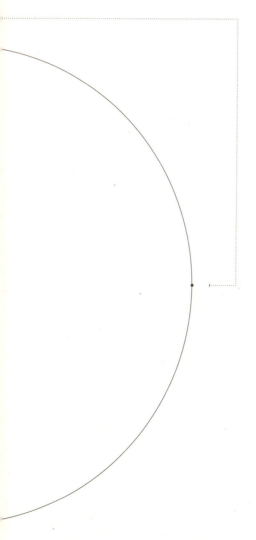

As you travel along the circle, from courage to humility,
you will make the required space for further impression.

Thus,
expression without impression will be empty. Impression
without expression will be carried out in vain.

Further,

if humility outweighs courage, you may lose the necessary connection to the self,[11] which can prove harmful. If courage outweighs humility, you may be unable to integrate the other into yourself, which can prevent you from connecting to the other.

Without such cycling between humility and courage, empathic conversation will be a significant challenge.

[11] Psychiatrist Carl Rogers famously said "...it is crucial that the therapist is able to perceive the experience of a person, but without losing the 'as if' the counselor were the client." If you go over the boundaries, it can negatively affect your mental well-being. For example, in the story I presented in the Prologue, the psychiatrist I met at the local support group suggested that I seek professional help, because she was worried that I might get pulled into my friend's depression while trying to empathize with her.

When the right balance of both humility and
courage is struck, what arises in their intersection
is a sense of resilient curiosity.

humility   *resilient*   *courage*
        curiosity

Being curious means that you trust that there's
something about the other that you do not know,
and despite not knowing what that may be,
you care enough to act in order to learn them,
because you trust that there's value in learning it.

Being resiliently curious means that despite the resistance
you experience while exercising your curiosity,
you do not give up.

_{Patience is also a part of this.}

As a matter of fact,
these challenges are the very things
that motivate you to want to persist.

But that's not all.

It also means
that you learn from each resistance,
so that when you give it another go,
you take the resistance into account
by having reconsidered your course of action.

What matters to a curious person is not whether she is
right or wrong, whether she agrees or disagrees, but
whether she can
learn about the other.
Whether she can
empathize with the other.
Whether she can
understand the other.

*And it is in this very process of trying to achieve these goals,
that she develops her sensitivity, knowledge,
and the skills needed*

to realize
her empathy

in relation to as many different others, in as many
different contexts as possible. ▪

To espouse humility is against the popular current.
We have lived in an atmosphere where the emphasis
has been increasingly on the use of force
and the assertion of the individual
—often leading to contradictions which actually deprive him
of his individual rights. Our philosophy has produced, and in
turn is the product of, the concepts of John Locke, Darwin,
Karl Marx, Nietzsche, and Freud. To discuss their political
exponents, the 20th-century mass killers and dictators, is
beyond the scope of this article. From these philosophers
emerge concepts of "survival of the fittest," the supremacy
of force, the advocacy of the assertion of brute instincts and
uninhibited actions emanating from the "unconscious," the
"rightful" domination of the "super-man."

W. HORSELY GANTT / PSYCHOLOGIST

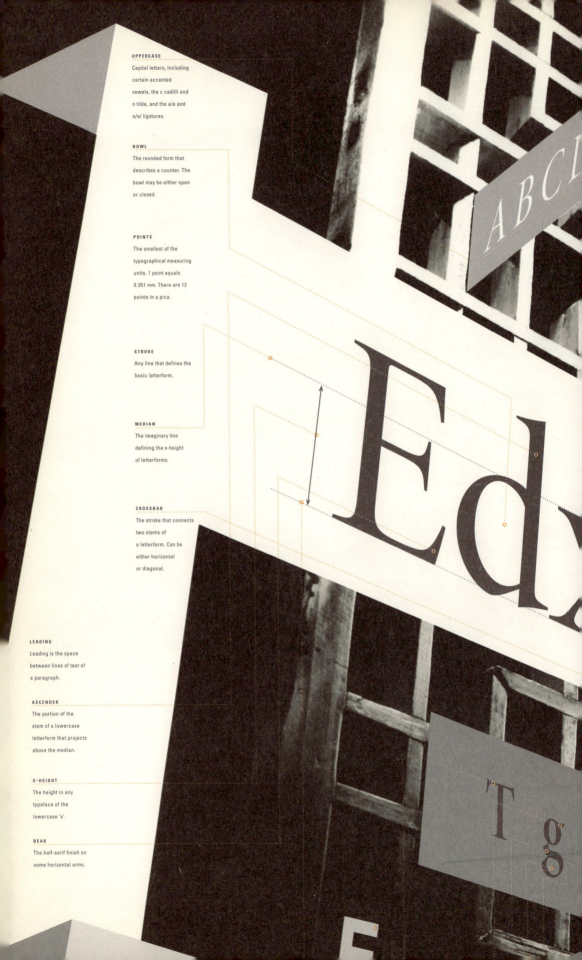

UPPERCASE
Capital letters, including certain accented vowels, the c cedilli and n tilde, and the a/e and o/e/ ligatures.

BOWL
The rounded form that describes a counter. The bowl may be either open or closed.

POINTS
The smallest of the typographical measuring units. 1 point equals 0.351 mm. There are 12 points in a pica.

STROKE
Any line that defines the basic letterform.

MEDIAN
The imaginary line defining the x-height of letterforms.

CROSSBAR
The stroke that connects two stems of a letterform. Can be either horizontal or diagonal.

LEADING
Leading is the space between lines of text of a paragraph.

ASCENDER
The portion of the stem of a lowercase letterform that projects above the median.

X-HEIGHT
The height in any typeface of the lowercase 'x'.

BEAK
The half-serif finish on some horizontal arms.

SMALL CAPS
Typeface style where all the letterforms take the shape of its capital letter.

CONDENSED
A condendsed version of the Roman form.

LIGHT
A lighter stroke than the Roman form. Even lighter strokes are often called 'thin'.

SPINE
The curved stem of the S.

CROSS STROKE
The horizontal stroke in a letterform that intersects the stem.

SWASH
The flourish that extends the stroke of a letterform.

LEG
Short stroke off the stem of the letterform, either at the bottom of the stroke (L) or inclined downward (K, R).

LOWERCASE NUMERALS
These numerals are set to x-height with ascenders and descenders. Also called oldstyle figures.

CROTCH
The interior space where two strokes meet.

STRESS
The orientation of the letterform, indicated by the thin stroke in round forms.

FINIAL
The rounded non-serif terminal to a stroke.

X-HEIGHT
The height in any typeface of the lowercase 'x'.

BEAK
The half-serif finish on some horizontal arms.

BASELINE
The imaginary line defining the visual base of letterforms.

BOLDFACE
Characterized by a thicker stroke than the roman form.

LOWERCASE
Lowercase letters including the same characters as uppercase plus f/i, f/l, f/f, f/f/i, and f/f/l ligatures, and the esset (German double s).

DINGBAT
An ornament, character or spacer used in typesetting, sometimes known as a "printer's ornament" or "printer's character".

INCORRECT LEADING
Be like water making its way through cracks. Do not be assertive, but adjust to the object, and you shall find a way around or through it.

EAR
The stroke extending out from the main stem or body of the letterform.

LINK
The stroke that connects the bowl and the loop of a lowercase 'g.'

LOOP
In some typefaces, the bowl created in the descender of the lowercase 'g.'

CORRECT LEADING
Be like water making its way through cracks. Do not be assertive, but adjust to the object, and you shall find a way around or through it.

TERMINAL
The self-contained finish of a stroke without a serif.

ARM
Short strokes off the stem of the letterform, either horizontal (E, F, T) or inclined upward (K, Y).

TAIL
The curved or diagonal stroke at the finish of certain letterforms.

CAP HEIGHT
The distance from the top of the capital to its bottom.

STRESS
The orientation of the letterform, indicated by the thin stroke in round forms.

FINIAL
The rounded non-serif terminal to a stroke.

LIGATURE
The characer formed by the combination of two or more letterforms.

EXTENDED
An extended variation on the Roman form.

PICA
Unit of measurement equivalent to 4.216 mm.

ITALIC
Named for the 14th century Italian handwriting on which the forms were based.

LINING FIGURES
A modern style of numerals where all figures are of the same height and rest on the baseline.

BARB
The half-serif finish on some curved strokes.

SPUR
The extension that articulates the juction of a curved and rectilinear stroke.

DESCENDER
That portion of the stem of a lowercase letterform that projects below the baseline.

ROMAN TYPE
Roman type stems from the stylistic origin of text typefaces from inscriptional capitals used in ancient Rome.

APEX/VERTEX
The point created by joining two diagonal stems (apex above, vertex below).

BRACKET
The transition between the serif and the stem.

SERIF
The right-angled or oblique foot at the end of the stroke.

EM
An em is the distance equal to the size of the typeface (an em in 48pt. type is 48 points, for example). An en is half the size of an em.

STEM
The significant vertical or oblique stroke.

COUNTER
The 'hollow' space of a letterform that is enclosed by the bowl.

SEUNG CHAN LIM
The designer of this poster. He designed the poster during his study at the Rhode Island School of Design in the year 2009.

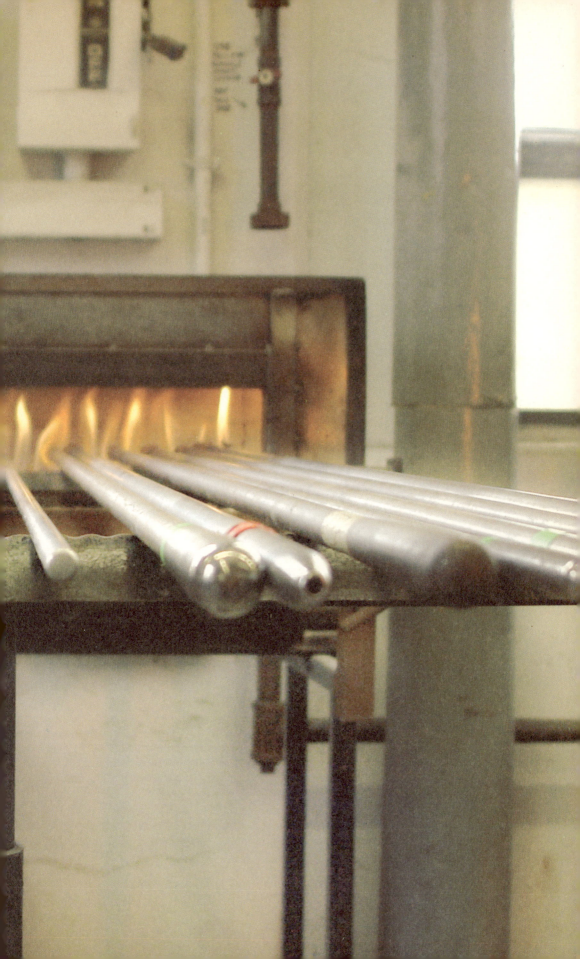

SLIM It's interesting to note that Guttenberg had to invent a number of things before the printing revolution occurred.

1. Metal type. (Metal type was invented in Korea ages before this point, but he didn't know about it.)
2. Ink that stays on metal.
3. The press.
4. The Bible printed using these technologies.

If the movable types were components of a platform that is the press, perhaps the ink was a kind of a glue, and the bible was a demonstration of its power that resonated with the masses. What are the necessary and sufficient conditions for a paradigm shift, I wonder?

When I listen to a classical piece of music, I see the players... vividly. I can envision their emotions right in front of my eyes. Their body movements, their facial expressions... Are there pieces of modern electronic music that will allow me to have such an experience?
Or has the focus shifted to just the music? Perhaps we don't value this much at all anymore? Have we ever?

March 4, 2009 10:38 p.m.

April 18, 2009 8:49 p.m.

FACILITATING EMPATHY

To demand, or to even ask someone

to realize their empathy, to engage in an empathic conversation,
                              can itself be considered non-empathic.
               Reflecting on the last chapter, I'm sure you can imagine how
               challenging it can be for someone to realize their empathy.

             And yet,
                    if you're a practitioner of empathic conversations
                 —whether you call it that or not—
                         it is common to feel that you would like to share this
                         experience with others, such that they can also benefit.

             So what are we to do?

One thing we can do is to proactively facilitate
and empower her to engage in empathic
conversations. In other words, we can design
for empathic conversations.
And we do this is by paying attention to the three
inextricable dimensions of empathic conversation:

The space occupied by the participants.   1

The attitude of the participants.   2

The language used by the participants.   3

Whether the facilitation is between her and yourself,
her and a computer, her and a piece of raw material,
her and her limbs, as long as there is her in relation
to an other, the same basic principles apply.

space

There is not a perfect word that I can use to refer to what I mean by "space." Some may wish to call it "context" or "atmosphere," while others prefer "place," "environment," or "platform."

Some may even wish to just call it "relationship."

But to put it simply,
a space in this context refers to the medium that participants can occupy and/or inhabit with others for the purpose of engaging in a conversation.

self

The analysis of bodily space has led us to results which may be generalized. We notice for the first time, with regard to our own body, what is true of all perceived things; that the perception of space and the perception of the thing, the spatiality of the thing and its being as a thing are not two distinct problems... To be a body, is to be tied to a certain world, as we have seen; our body is not primarily in space, it is of it.

MAURICE MERLEAU-PONTY / PHILOSOPHER

But it's less important that we have a precise definition of space. What's important is to make clear that what I mean by space is not simply what is in between the walls of buildings. Whenever there is a self and other in relationship, they are occupying a space.

A house that has been experienced is not an inert box.
Inhabited space transcends geometrical space.

GASTON BACHELARD / PHILOSOPHER

Remember the last time you were reading a really
good fiction book. The space between yourself
and the characters is just as much a space as the
kind that is in between the walls of buildings.

> The fact is Middle-earth is more real to me than many "actual"
> places; and if I should suddenly find myself there (which would
> of course astound me—but not utterly) I would have a better
> feeling for it, and a better idea of how to find my way about, than
> if I had been dropped in, say, central Asia or South America.
> **PATRICK CURRY / WRITER**

To put it more plainly, the significance of space in the
context of designing for empathic conversations, lies
primarily in the fact that spaces embody qualities that are
perceptible and memorable.
other

> [The] unity of space can be discovered only in the interplay
> of the sensory realms. That is what remains true in the
> celebrated empiricist description of a non-spatial perception.
> The experience of persons blind from birth and operated upon
> for cataract has never proved, and could never prove, that for
> them space begins with sight.
> **MAURICE MERLEAU-PONTY / PHILOSOPHER**

Just as architects arrange the walls so as to give rise to
a variety of different spaces between them, designing
for empathic conversation entails arranging the
participants so as to give rise to a space between them
that they perceive as being sufficiently dynamic and
intimate for empathic conversation.

Now then,
what do I mean by dynamic and intimate?

Imagine a room you consider to be spacious. Feel how the spaciousness of the room directly impacts your ability to act freely and purposefully, to move from one perspective to another, and to form different relationships with other occupants in the space. To perceive of one's potential to creatively, spontaneously, and continuously realize such abilities is to perceive of the potential for dynamism[1] in a given space.[2]

[1] Dynamism is often misunderstood as a synonym for something wildly crazy, but what it signifies is simply the qualities embodied in our interaction with mother nature, such as open-endedness, continual change, and spontaneity. For a more in-depth treatment of the idea of dynamism, take a look at Virginia Postrel's *The Future and Its Enemies*.

> Not only do many homesick women report being claustrophobic, the intensity of the claustrophobic feelings seem to vary with the intensity of the feeling of homesickness also. In the homesick the enclosed spaces are feared because escape is difficult or impossible. They express the need to be able to go home whenever they want to... Typically claustrophobic experiences are not reported at home; as the fear is not related to the small space but rather to the inability to go home.
>
> MIRANDA VAN TILBURG / HEALTH PSYCHOLOGIST

[2] As a counter-example, imagine being inside a crowded subway.

Whether the desired act of freedom and purpose is decorating the space with your own choice of furniture, making a mess building a plaster cast of a large piece of sculpture, or engaging in a lively and thought-provoking discussion, if a space does not hint at the appropriate potential for dynamism, it will be unlikely to be perceived as valuable or safe enough for empathic conversation.

Now, imagine a room you consider to be your own private sanctuary. Feel how the safety of the room directly impacts your ability to reveal your vulnerability, and to feel confident enough to take risks.

> Trust, faith that confidences will not be betrayed and privileged knowledge will not be used against the self, is perhaps a more fundamental dimension of intimacy than knowing and understanding as these terms are now used.
>
> LYNN JAMIESON / SOCIOLOGIST

To perceive of one's potential to freely and purposefully
realize such abilities is to perceive of the potential
for intimacy[3]
in a given space.[4]

Whether the risk involves the potential for physical
harm, shame, embarrassment, or loss of reputation,
if a space does not hint at the appropriate potential
for intimacy, it will be unlikely to be perceived as
valuable or safe enough for empathic conversation.

It's useful to talk about the perception of intimacy and
dynamism in two separate stages. The first stage is
when you have no prior experience of the space, and
second is when you do. It's important to consider the
first stage of perception in case you're inviting someone
to occupy a space unfamiliar to them. Whatever
language you're using to give them a first impression,
if they do not perceive any intimacy or dynamism at
this stage, they may not wish to occupy the space.

Remember the story I shared with you in the Preface?
The woodshop, at that time, was not a space I perceived
as being either dynamic or intimate, so I was rather
hesitant to occupy it. The only reason I was there was
because I trusted the advice of the student enough
to assume that some value was to be had from this
occupation. But now that I have not only acquired the
skill to make furniture, but also come to genuinely
love carpentry, I perceive great levels of intimacy and
dynamism whenever I visit.

The same applies to our interaction with the computer.

Say you're face-to-face with a laptop computer, and
you're completely unaware of anything other than
yourself and the computer. At that moment,
you and the computer
are the two occupants of a space.

---

[3] Many people take intimacy to mean something of a sexual nature. While that can certainly be a part of it, as it is discussed in the field of psychotherapy, levels of intimacy is simply the degree to which one reveals one's self honestly, casually referred to as "into me see."

[4] As a counter-example, imagine being amidst complete strangers in a foreign city.

Now,
if you have never heard of or a computer before or have limited experience using one, it is unlikely that you will be aware of what potential for dynamism or intimacy lies in your sustained occupation of this space. So unless the form of the computer hints at its potential for dynamism and intimacy, it is unlikely that you will have the motivation to further occupy this space.

> [Steve] Jobs kept insisting that the [first Macintosh] should look friendly. As a result, it evolved to resemble a human face. With the disk drive below the screen, the unit was taller and narrower than most computers, suggesting a head...Oyama later said, "To be honest, we didn't know what it meant for a computer to be 'friendly' until Steve told us."
> WALTER ISAACSON / WRITER

On the other hand,
if you're a skilled and passionate programmer, with substantial experience with this kind of laptop computer, even without any external indication, you can probably imagine a variety of software programs you can develop on it,[5] enough to motivate you to want to occupy the space further. Whether this is in relation to the computer hardware or the screen provided by a software application, the same principles apply.

[5] This isn't to say that programming skills are necessary to imagine the potential for dynamism and intimacy in a computational space. An expert Adobe Photoshop user, a professional blogger, or a gamer may be just as capable.

> I still remember the first time I saw the screen for Adobe After Effects. Talk about a lack of dynamism and intimacy on first impression.

As you can see, attributes such as your skills can affect your attitude, which in turn determines our perception of dynamism and intimacy in a given space.

In fact,
in the case of my woodshop story in the Preface, even if I could not perceive enough dynamism or intimacy, I was able to compensate for it by proactively employing a level of humility and courage in relation to the advice I was given from a student. In much the same way, you may decide to occupy a space with no perceptible affordance of dynamism or intimacy, by proactively trusting that such potential can arise in the future.

So when inviting someone to occupy a space, it is
important that you have enough understanding
of their attitude,
in order to consider a language
that facilitates their perception of dynamism
and intimacy, sufficient enough for them to find
it valuable and safe enough for occupation.

> [At] the heart of sustaining desire in a committed relationship, is the reconciliation of two fundamental human needs. On the one hand, our need for security, for predictability, for safety, for dependability, for reliability, for permanence—all these anchoring, grounding experiences of our lives that we call home. But we also have an equally strong need—men and women —for adventure, for novelty, for mystery, for risk, for danger, for the unknown, for the unexpected, surprise—you get the gist—for journey, for travel.
>
> **ESTHER PEREL / PSYCHOLOGIST**

Dynamism

Interesting | Appealing

Meaningless / Intimidating | Comforting

First Impression | Intimacy

Let's assume that we were able to get past the first stage, and people have occupied the space. Now their perception of the space will start to change as they interact with the other occupants of the space. So just as we aimed to provide a perceptible potential for dynamism and intimacy in the space prior to their occupation, we now have to do the same during their occupation of the space.

How do we do this, you ask?

By modeling to them, a sufficient degree
of honesty, sincerity, and integrity.

self

honesty

Honesty is the central axis with respect to which empathic conversations
revolve.
If raw materials were dishonest, craftsmen would have a significantly more difficult time engaging in an empathic conversation with them.

No matter what kind of language we use,
if it is not used to express honesty, the other will have difficulty forming a clear and accurate understanding of our expressions. Without such understandings, the other will either find it difficult to realize their empathy in relation to us, or be misled into believing that they have.

In either case, dishonesty will negatively affect the other's ability to trust or to act freely in relation to us, making it less likely that they will perceive the necessary and sufficient potential for dynamism and intimacy in the space.

But modeling honesty is difficult.
Because what we need to be honest about, and to what degree or scale, depends largely on the context.

Take the example from our interaction with the computer. When you ask Adobe Illustrator to measure in inches, more often than not
it will lie.[6]
Despite labeling its view "Actual Size" shown at "100%," the rulers will merely claim to measure in inches, without actually doing so.[7]

[6] Technically speaking, the designers of Adobe Illustrator have designed it to do so.

But an inch is not an abstract concept. It has meaning in relation to our bodies. Merely notating something as such does not make it so.

[7] When the document is printed, this, of course, gets rectified. But the lack of honesty still remains on screen.

The side margin of this book is 2.5 inches.

Now, you may be thinking to yourself, "But I don't care," and that's partly why honesty is so difficult.

Honesty is relational.

You don't care because you don't have the need or the desire to reconcile the dissonance[8] between what you imagined your design would look like when printed, and what it actually looks like when printed. Once again, what we need to be honest about, and to what degree or scale, depends largely on the context.

[8] For an example of a group of people who do have such a need, talk to graphic designer whose work involves a great deal of printed posters or books.

Here's another example.
The scale of honesty desired by those who program in low-level languages such as C or Assembly are often different from those who program in high-level languages such as JavaScript. The difference could be more easily understood using the analogy of a material scientist versus an industrial designer or an architect.

Those who engineer materials care about a clear and accurate understanding of the structures of physical matter dealing with concepts such as atoms and molecules or crystal structures and density.[9]

[9] So if you're trying to facilitate an empathic conversation between a raw material and a material scientist, you will want to provide them with the tools they need to get to this scale of honesty.

This is because they know that their ignorance to such low-level understandings can lead to the production of materials that introduce greatly magnified problems for those who work with their materials at a higher level.

Similarly,
those who program at low-levels care about a clear and accurate understanding of the structures of computational matter dealing with concepts such as bits and bytes or hardware instructions and memory addresses.

This is because they know that their ignorance to such low-level understandings can lead to greatly magnified problems for scripters[10] and software architects at a higher level.

On the other hand,
those who program in high-level languages are similar to industrial designers or architects in the sense that they care mostly about the resulting properties of these materials, so as to gauge whether they'd be appropriate for use in their projects. For them, such low-level of honesty may be considered
    too much information.

Then there is the fact that
even if you have no intention to deceive,
    the other may still feel that you lack honesty.

Take the fact that the computer stores data in what is called memory. Some are meant to be temporary like those stored in Random Access Memory (RAM), while others more permanent like those stored in a hard disk or a thumb drive. A seasoned user of Windows or Mac OS X knows that when her computer starts to act in a sluggish manner, it is usually to do with running out of space for memory. So as she starts to experience sluggishness, she may open an application like Task Manager or Activity Monitor to find out how much space is left.

---

[10] Those who program in high-level languages are commonly referred to as "scripters."

And since these software programs
honestly display this information,
she can consider an adequate response by
quitting applications or deleting unwanted
files, in order to make more space.

But let's say that before she could open these software
programs, her cursor turns into an hour glass or a spinning
beach ball, and the computer becomes unresponsive. Now
what? One might be tempted to defend the computer by
saying that it no longer has the ability to realize its potential
for honesty. While this is true from the perspective of the
computer, as far as she is concerned, she is expressing
interest in knowing
—even if it means randomly pressing buttons on the keyboard or
the mouse—
yet the computer is refusing to respond. As a result,
she can feel frustrated and sometimes even betrayed
because she feels that the computer is withholding
information from her.

In essence,
there is a misunderstanding. So this means that to
prevent such misunderstandings, we also have to be
proactively honest.

For example, one of the root causes of the previous problem
deals with the fact that the computer is not proactively honest
about the spatial limitations of its memory. What does this
mean? Imagine how you would feel if your stomach was not
proactively honest about its spatial limits, if we did not feel
full until the very last moment, the moment right before your
stomach is about to burst. Or how about if our rooms would
not give out any indication of how full they are, until you get
suffocated to death. We would think it's ridiculous.

And yet,
this is not too different from what happens in our
interaction with Windows or Mac OS X when we
run out of hard drive space all of a sudden.

But the problem is that
to predict what to be proactively honest about
and to what degree or scale is a significant challenge. To be able to do so would mean that we are omniscient. After all, how are we to know when we're being misunderstood by others or know what their expectations are with respect to the scale of honesty desired?

Hell, most of the times we don't even know when we're being dishonest to ourselves.

But that's not all.
Remember the story of me in the woodshop sawing a piece of wood. It doesn't matter how honest we think we are if the other isn't listening. Also, remember the story of me and my poster. Even if the professor is being honest, if the language used is ill-considered, the other cannot understand the intended meaning.

As you can see, even without any intent to deceive, honesty can be very difficult to model in relation to an other. If we take into consideration other elements such as fear, and vulnerability, which can cause intentional dishonesty, it can seem downright impossible to model honesty.

Thank God, raw materials do not have fear.

But the modeling of absolute honesty is not a requirement when designing for empathic conversations. What is required is that we model a degree of honesty, sufficient enough for the other to perceive
our sincere desire to be honest.

Although, what does that mean? To express a sincere desire to be honest? Is it like "good will"?

[Nothing] in the world is absolutely good without restriction, save a good will, and that this good will sets the limit to everything and for that reason is then good without limitation.
IMMANUEL KANT / PHILOSOPHER

Simply put, modeling a sincere desire to be honest means that not only are we not intentionally dishonest, but we are also doing our best to proactively prevent and remedy[11] misunderstandings that can arise from our inability to be absolutely honest.

In other words, instead of trying to model absolute honesty, we model however much honesty we deem appropriate, and model with it a level of proactive care[12] and willingness to be additionally honest[13] if needed.

> [In a farming framework defined by cura (care),] one has to care for the animals, the plants, the fields—and if work is done with care, then production per labor object will be high. Cura equals craftsmanship. It refers to the quality of labor or, in more general terms, to ordering the processes of production and reproduction in such a way as to guarantee that good yields and steady increases are the outcome.
>
> **JAN DOUWE VAN DER PLOEG / SOCIAL SCIENTIST**

Because when such sincerity is perceived, and there is an ongoing facilitation of empathic conversation, the misunderstandings will likely be resolved through the very process of empathic conversation.

Remember what my friend was able to do in the acting class? If the director was not skilled at facilitating empathic conversations, that would not have been possible. The acting teachers I've met go out of their way to model sincerity. They regularly and honestly shared their vulnerable personal stories with their students. They were always themselves, and rarely tried to appear like a "teacher." They honestly demonstrated their acting abilities to their students. They joined the students in making embarrassing bodily noises during warm-up.

And the outcome of such sincerity was that the level of intimacy and dynamism the students felt in the space was extraordinary. And when they were asked to "take risks," they did so in ways you would never be able to imagine.[14]

---

[11] The idea of tact and honesty is worth mentioning here as well. Many think they are being "honest," when in fact they are merely being hurtful. The problem isn't so much the fact that you're hurting the other, but that that's all you may be doing. In other words, because the other feels hurt, your honesty is not actually being communicated. The purpose of honesty in empathic conversation isn't being honest fo the sake of being honest, it is to serve the purpose of realizing both you and other's empathy. Sincerity includes such consideration for tact in addition to honesty.

[12] One can think of the level of craftsmanship an object embodies to be directly related to the sincerity embodied by the craftsman when making the object.

[13] Raw materials are incapable of being proactive and therefore cannot express sincerity. On the other hand, there is no reason why we cannot design the computer to do so. Yet, very few software allows for such possibility. For example, a friend of mine had an advertisement show up on her Facebook soliciting her to be an adult model. Another time, she was asked to buy weight-loss products. She wanted to find out what exactly about the way she used Facebook lead to this targeting. She didn't just want to "report the ad," she wanted to resolve the root of the misunderstanding. But, of course, no such thing is possible.

[14] In college, Dr. Randy Pausch told me that I should take an acting class. I didn't listen to him, of course. I didn't have the knowledge to understand what it meant "to take an acting class." I now go around telling other people to take an acting class. They don't listen to me, either.

CHAPTER 4

What we also do by modeling such sincerity, is that we not only facilitate their development of a clear and accurate understanding of our expressions, but also how we are in general.

In other words, by disclosing the kinds of constraints and vulnerabilities we need to disclose to prevent misunderstandings, **we demystify ourselves,** and empower the other to perceive beyond our superficial differences, and toward the underlying similarities.

self

> In the face of [our difference to others] our similarity often comes into focus. Defining "us" involves defining a range of "thems" also. When we say something about others we are often saying something about ourselves. In the human world, similarly and difference are always functions of a point of view: our similarity is their difference and vice versa. Similarity and difference reflect each other across a shared boundary. At the boundary, we discover what we are in what we are not, and vice versa.
> RICHARD JENKINS / SOCIOLOGIST

honesty

[15] This is one of the things that happened when I took the class on Computer Architecture. Realizing the physicality of the computer and the fact that it has limitations not only helped me understand it better, but it also made it more relatable than before.

In fact, finding such similarities in relation to us, to find a small piece of themselves in us, —no matter how minor— will help them identify[15] with us, which ultimately serves to develop their sense of identity in relation to us,[16] in turn,

> [In] the psychoanalytic tradition, both persons and things are tellingly called "objects" ... For Freud, when we lose a beloved person or object, we begin a process that, if successful, ends in our finding them again, within us. It is, in fact, how we grow and develop as people... The psychodynamic tradition—in its narrative of how we make objects part of ourselves—offers a language for interpreting the intensity of our connections to the world of things
> SHERRY TURKLE / SOCIOLOGIST

dignity

[16] Have you ever felt that you were like a "different person" depending on who you were with at any given moment?

affecting their perception of intimacy and dynamism in relation to us.

What also affects their sense of identity in
relation to us is our willingness to be sincere
in a timely manner.

> [Much] of reacting is timing, and timing grows
> out of what the character is going through.
> LARRY MOSS / ACTING COACH

When our desire to interact fails to generate a reaction
within an expected range of time, we feel a sense of doubt,
confusion, or frustration. Whether it's our angry significant
others not reacting to our plea for conversation, our e-mails
not being replied to, or no amount of moving the mouse or
typing on the keyboard will get the computer to react, the
same principles apply.

By reacting to the other's actions in a timely manner,
we reinforce their basic need to matter. Such closure
of a feedback loop
—no matter how mundane—
affirms their sense of self, of existence, of dignity,
which, once again, affects our perception of
intimacy and dynamism in relation to the other.

> Dignity is a paradoxical word. When we pay heed to the dignity
> of others, we do it for the sake of their immeasurable singularity.
> And yet, the unique value we impute to them makes it seem as
> though they alone carried the infinite worth of all humanity.
> DRUCILLA CORNELL / PROFESSOR OF POLITICAL SCIENCE

[17] It's significant that I'm using the word "sense" to describe integrity. Because that's what matters. If you cannot sense an other's integrity, then you cannot trust it.

[18] The sense of trust that comes from experiencing an other's integrity is trust earned, which is to be distinguished from the kind of blind trust you give during team-building exercises where you're asked to fall down with your eyes closed hoping that the others will succeed at catching you.

[19] Implying trust in their own skills, sensitivities, and knowledge in relation to us.

[20] If you think back to the story of me trying to tear glass, I did not have enough experience with glass to have developed a sufficient sense of integrity, which meant that there was a fair amount of distance between myself and glass, because there was not a trust relationship. This also made it easy for me to want to blame it for being different, difficult, and unpredictable.

Now if we can consistently model such honesty and sincerity over time, what starts to arise in their general understanding of how we are is a sense[17] of integrity.

In other words, we will have demonstrated to them a sufficiently discernible structure, pattern, and property in the way we act or react, enough to empower them to trust[18] us.
And not just trust us,
but also
trust themselves[19] in relation to us,
thereby reducing the perceived distance between the self and the other.[20]

Without such sense of integrity, the craftsman will have a significantly different relationship with his materials.

It's easy to say that all that lies at the heart of his ability to do this is the belief that they can predict our future actions in relation to their own. That we will continue to act in manners consistent with their understanding of how we are. While that is certainly a large portion of it, there is more to this sense of trust than mere predictability.

For example, once they have developed a sufficient sense of trust in us,
when their prediction proves wrong,
and we act in ways that seem inconsistent with their understanding of how we are, they will be far more willing to wonder how they could integrate and reconcile this new behavior into their current understanding of us.

In other words, if we cannot model a sufficient degree of integrity enough to develop a sense of resiliency in their trust in relation to us, they are more likely to assume that we are not trustworthy, and never bother to give us the benefit of doubt, or try to engage in an empathic conversation with us to resolve the perceived discrepancy.

No matter how much we try, it is unlikely that we can achieve perfection. Not only because it is difficult to achieve perfection, but also because the sense of integrity and trust we're talking about is, once again, relational.

Take the story of me in the metal shop as an example. I was about to assume that metal was different from wood in that it was dishonest. Assuming this would naturally affect my ability to trust it. However, it turns out there was a misunderstanding. The brick was affecting my perception of the metal. If it weren't for my friend who resolved the misunderstanding for me, I may have been unable to feel a sufficient sense of trust in metals for the rest of my life.

But there is one more element to the development of such sense of trust. And that is **the blurring of the boundary** between one's self and the other.

I once took an architecture class, where I was assigned to draft six highly-detailed plans and elevations big enough to fill a giant sheet of vellum as tall and as wide as myself. This was the first time in my life learning how to draft, so I naturally felt overwhelmed by the sheer scale of the drawings I had to complete.

Thankfully, we were given a tutorial on how to use the mayline, the protractors, the rulers, and the lead holders, and it didn't seem too bad.

CHAPTER 4

honesty

But what surprised me the most,
was that when I sat down and started to draft, I felt as if I had been there before. I felt as if I were home. I felt assured. I felt that I was occupying
a rather intimate and dynamic space.

To be clear, the assignment was still overwhelming. But my interaction with the tools was something different. I would go in so far as to say that I felt as if I had the means to draw anything I wanted.[21]

[21] Not that I actually could, but that I felt as if I could. I also get the same feeling when I sit down to program in my favorite programming language, but that took me a really long time to get there.

It is, of course, difficult to pinpoint exactly why this was, but I felt as if I had a clear enough understanding of the abilities and constraints of the tools I was using to draft, to envision what I could and could not do in relation to them. And not only that, but the scale and stance of the drafting board in relation to my body, how I was able to position my body in relation to it, the immediacy of using the rulers to measure things, to feel the firm and tactile feedback of the lead holders rubbing against the vellum, all seemed to play a role in helping me
forget
that I was drafting for the first time.

In other words,
I felt as if I could trust both myself as well as the others in the space, enough to stop thinking about
*the other as the other,
and the self as the self.*
As such conscious differentiation of the self and the other started to dissolve into the space, I was able to feel a sense of dynamism and intimacy in the space.

[Loss] of self-consciousness does not involve a loss of self, and certainly not a loss of consciousness, but rather only a loss of consciousness of the self. What slips below the threshold of awareness is the concept of self, the information we use to represent to ourselves who we are... This feeling is not just a fancy of the imagination, but is based on a concrete experience of close interaction with some other, an interaction that produces a rare sense of unity with these usually foreign entities.

MIHALY CSIKSZENTMIHALYI / PSYCHOLOGIST

In much the same way, when an other develops a sufficient sense of trust in relation to us, we empower them to lose their sense of self-consciousness in relation to us, as long as we do not violate[22] this sense of trust.

[22] A software crash taking with it hours' worth of work is a great example of such violation of trust.

> [The] hardest earned and most fragile accomplishment of childhood, basic trust, can be damaged beyond repair by trauma. Human beings are surrounded by layers of trust, radiating out in concentric circles like the ripples in a pond. The experience of trauma, at its worst, can mean not only a loss of confidence in the self, but a loss of confidence in the surrounding tissue of family and community, in the structures of human government, in the larger logics by which humankind lives, in the ways of nature itself, and often (if this is really the final step in such a succession) in God.
>
> KAI ERIKSON / SOCIOLOGIST

Now, let's finally take a moment to talk about the importance of language.

Language is what is used to model all the above mentioned concepts like honesty, sincerity, and integrity. In other words, without language, none of these qualities can be perceived by the other.

As you may have guessed, to say that a language is required when designing for empathic conversation is not to say that the written or the spoken language must be provided. In fact, a language can be made of any media capable of being expressed and perceived as stimuli by the participants of the conversation.

Remember the story of me in the woodshop.
By using the saw, I was able to express to a piece of wood, what I meant by "to cut a notch." The saw was a part of the language I used to converse with the wood.

I could have also used another tool to say the same thing.

For example, I was using a double-blade saw at the time, but I could have used a backsaw[23] instead. But people who care about quality will say that the notch I get using the two different saws are not "the same thing." The two kinds of notches that get cut are significantly different, because the backsaw gives more clarity, precision, and accuracy in making the cut.[24]

I suppose a master may be able to get the same cut despite the difference in tools.

In other words, depending on your choice of language, the clarity, precision, and accuracy with which you communicate your meaning will vary. And no matter what meaning you embody, what is ultimately perceived by the other is the language you use.

> [Consider] the meaning of the word "communication." This is based on the Latin "commun" and the suffix "ie" which is similar to "fie," in that it means "to make or to do." So one meaning of "to communicate" is to "to make something common," i.e., to convey information or knowledge from one person to another in as accurate a way as possible.
>
> DAVID BOHM / PHYSICIST

But beyond mere clarity, accuracy, and precision, even the basic meaning can be completely lost if you choose the wrong language.

Think of the language used by the wood.
The sound it made, the feeling of resistance it gave against the saw, the wood debris it generated, the gap that was created in its place, these were all part of its language. But the problem with that language was that it was a language I was unable to make meaning from.

---

[23] A saw whose web is stiffened by a metallic back of greater substance.

[24] Although it wouldn't have helped me too much given the horrible clamping job I had done.

Now, it's absurd to think that languages are inherently meaningful. If this were true, we should be able to listen to any foreign language, and instantly understand it. So it should be no surprise that one has to learn the language[25] in order to make meaning from it. Which means the question comes down to "can I?" and "will I?"

For example, if I have the time and energy to do it that would be a start. But do I also have the skills needed to respect and listen? After all, I failed to do so in relation to glass and wood. Do I have the necessary knowledge and sensitivity? I don't think I would have been able to learn about the brick without my friend.

In other words, if the "foreignness" of the language is inappropriate for the knowledge, sensitivity, and skill that make up one's attitude, it will be insufficient for empathic conversation, because they will have a difficult time communicating, which will frustrate them, and in turn affect their perception of intimacy and dynamism in the space.

So when choosing a language to facilitate an empathic conversation, regardless of what form it takes, it matters greatly that it is capable of facilitating a sufficiently clear, accurate, and precise exchange *of meaning,* and that its foreignness is appropriate for the attitude they bring to the space.

[25] In fact, just because we both speak English, it doesn't mean we speak the same language. We still have to learn each other's languages.

> [The] exchange of meaning is problematic... it is affected by social organization and social structure... individuals and groups struggle over the forms, processes, and content of communication... a presumption of consensus or shared meaning is frequently erroneous... The studies emphasizing negotiation demonstrate that taken-for-granted symbols are frequently the subject of disagreement. The work of the social constructionists show that things like news and social problems, which everyone assumes to be "hard" and objective, are human creations subject to differences of opinion and perception.
> PETER HALL / SOCIAL SCIENTIST

CHAPTER 4

Now then,
    how can we do this?

[26] This also happens frequently in relation to ourselves. We misunderstand ourselves to want X, when in fact we really want Y. But it isn't until we are able to empathize with ourselves that this misunderstanding gets resolved. But when it does get resolved, it becomes clear what we have to do.

Remember the story of me working on my poster?
    In the beginning I had a misunderstanding of what the instructor meant by "foreground" and "background." But the moment I had an experience I felt was similar enough to the one he had in mind, I was able to understand him. And when I understood him, what I had to do became extremely clear.[26] In the same way, what we need to provide as a way to facilitate an empathic conversation is
    a language composed of triggers capable of recalling the experiences shared by the participants.

In other words,
    to facilitate an empathic conversation,
    we need a language made up of metaphors.

Poetry the shortest distance between two humans.
    LAWRENCE FERLINGHETTI / POET

If I were to try and be more ideal,
    what we need is language consisting
of shared metaphors.
    And by shared metaphors, I mean metaphors capable
        of triggering sufficiently similar experiences
in all the participants
    of a given conversation.

At first glance, such shared metaphors may seem impossible to attain, but they are actually quite easy to come by when the participants have a history with one another.

For example, among long-time friends, even a single picture or a few words such as "our high school prom" can readily trigger a complex set of shared experiences among all those involved. At other times, you may witness a scene together and even without having to say anything, end up looking at each other with a knowing glance, because you know exactly what the other is thinking.

Such is the power of shared metaphors.

But if the participants do not have a history together, and we cannot know in advance what common experiences exist among them, all is not lost. We can still encourage them to converse with each other for the purpose of exploring what shared experiences exist, and provide them with a foundation from which they can co-evolve a set of shared metaphors.

A good example of such co-evolution can be found in the domain of human computer interaction under the name of macros.[27] For those unfamiliar with macros, you may also have heard it used under the name of "actions" found in Adobe Photoshop.

In essence, what you can do with macros is that you can ask the computer to observe and remember a long and complicated series of actions you take, then by giving this memory a label, you can later recall it from its memory, and have it reenacted verbatim.

In other words, the label becomes a shared metaphor between the computer and the person occupying the space.[28]

[27] Macros are used to make a sequence of computing instructions available to the programmer as a single program statement, making the programming task less tedious and less error-prone. (Greenwald, 1959, 132)

[28] Macros are often marketed as a means to increase productivity, but looked at from the perspective of an empathic conversation, such increased productivity is merely a side effect of the participants' ability to efficiently exchange meaning.

[29] You can think of part of what I've tried to do in this book, which is to share my stories with you, as following the very principles of shared metaphors. In other words, while you and I are physically apart, my telling of stories, through the power of empathy, creates a space occupied by you, me, and others to serve as a second-best way of sharing an experience. So phrases such as "remember the story of me sawing a piece of wood?" becomes a metaphor.

In the same way, to facilitate an empathic conversation among participants who do not share any experiences, you have to give them an opportunity to have a shared experience, and also provide them with the means to recall aspects of these experience using an agreed-upon trigger.[29] This will then become their shared language.

In fact,
even if there already exists a set of shared metaphors, such co-evolvability will still be needed to grow their shared language, to make them capable of expressing an ever-growing variety of meanings with increasing precision and accuracy.

A specific situation calls for a specific metaphor—none other—
each with its precision. To evaluate all these sorts of precision with
one sort—logico-mathematical, say—is unfair and imprecise...
Metaphor is not imprecise but precision-creative, ex-pressing
novelty dynamics, precisely expressing the chameleonic situation.

KUANG-MING WU / HERMENEUT

If the other is able to trust us enough to lose their sense of self-consciousness, and if we have the means to use and to co-evolve a set of shared metaphors to exchange meaning, what also starts to develop
is their skill of interaction
in relation to us.

In other words,
they get to become skillful at knowing what they can and cannot do with us, how their actions influence us and how ours influence them, and how to exchange meaning in as clear, accurate, and precise a way as possible. And it is through the acquisition of such skill that they will feel empowered to make things with us, to tell their own stories to and through us, to further achieve their sense
of dignity,
both in relation to us and beyond.

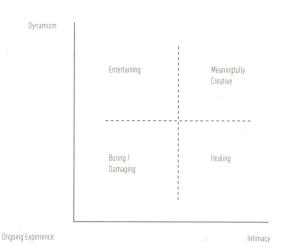

And the more they are able to make in
this fashion, the more they'll develop
their courage and humility,

> Here is how a dancer expresses this dimension of the flow experience: "A strong relation and calmness comes over me. I have no worries of failure. What a powerful and warm feeling it is! I want to expand, to hug the world. I feel enormous power to effect something of grace and beauty"... What [she] is describing is the possibility rather than the actuality, of control. The ballet dancer may fall, break her leg, and never make the perfect turn.... But at least in principle, in the world of flow perfection is attainable.
>
> **MIHALY CSIKSZENTMIHALYI / PSYCHOLOGIST**

which will empower them to diversify the kinds of others they will be willing to engage in empathic conversations with, increase the amount of dynamism and intimacy they perceive in relation to these various others, and help them develop the discipline needed to balance their awareness of self in relation to others.[30]

[30] This balance is crucial. To strike this balance is to not lose one's integrity, while trying to empathize with an other. For a therapist this can mean not becoming overwhelmed by the patient's emotions. For an actor, this can mean being able to clearly deliver the memorized lines in the midst of being immersed in intense emotion. For a communication designer, this can mean staying true to the content while still being considerate of the viewer.

To be clear, designing for empathic conversation cannot guarantee that the other will feel empowered to engage in an empathic conversation, although it can certainly raise the probability of them doing so.

At the same time, I can never emphasize enough that designing for empathic conversation is not an effort to "get" them to engage in empathic conversations, or to "change" them.

It would, of course, be great if everybody engaged in empathic conversations, and the same may be true with empowering others to experiencing change. But that is not the goal.

Rather,
the goal of designing for empathic conversation is to facilitate and to empower others to experience for themselves the value of engaging in an empathic conversation. And we do this
by providing a space
where we can share with them our modeling of honesty, sincerity, and integrity.

Any ulterior motives will simply get in the way of achieving this goal. ■

The computer is a "psychological machine." On the border between mind and not mind,
it invites its anthropomorphization, its psychologization. It does this almost universally, for children and grown-ups, men and women, novices and experts. This does not mean that people see it as "alive," but rather, there is a pull to psychologize the machine, to give it an intellectual and aesthetic personality. The computer facilitates **a relational encounter with a formal system.**

SHERRY TURKLE / SOCIOLOGIST

SLIM One of the most profound shifts in my thinking that has occurred in the past year (there have been quite a few) is that graphic designers and other visual artists such as printmakers and painters have long imagined an infinite space under the constraint of a two-dimensional medium such as the canvas and paper. Thus, part of the goal was to get us to forget that what we are seeing was a piece of paper or a canvas. This desire has given birth to a vast amount of knowledge base. We learned that color, scale, and others can all be used to depict spatial information, which translates to a sense of hierarchy and other feelings.

Now if that's the case, why is the world of software so obsessed with making sure that we see that things are printed on "paper." Most of the document editing software such as microsoft Word have this paradigm. And the use of the term "page" for the World Wide Web certainly has its roots in the printed paper. Interesting, no?

November 18, 2009, 2:16 a.m.

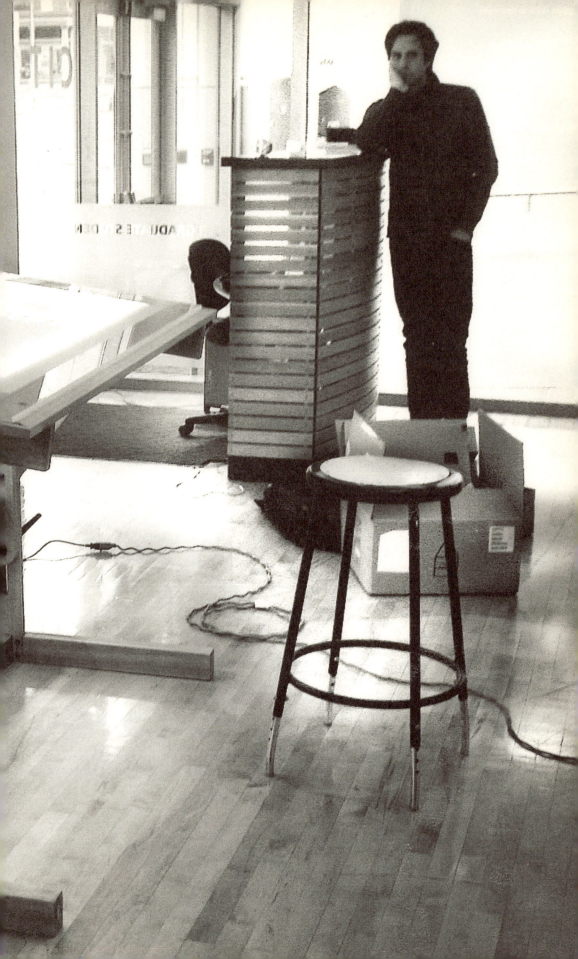

SLIM There are so many amazing conversations that go on in the physical world of making.

Just the simple act of trying to get a block of metal flattened creates an amazing exchange, as you are:

1. Sensing how parallel your file is to the surface of the metal
2. Observing how flat the surface really is by using a machinist's square
3. Observing what is getting filed, by the different reflection of light (you can also mark the surface with ink and you'll be able to do this in a different way)
4. Getting into a rhythm of filing that provides you a relatively consistent reference for measuring how much to file to get the result you'd like

December 2, 2009, 7:43 p.m.

DESIGN AND EMPATHY

As the final project in our acting class,

CHAPTER 5

my friend, who had played Blanche, performed a song she had written herself.
It was about the person she had remembered
on stage to act the role of Blanche.

Before she began to sing, she carefully and candidly
shared with us who this person was, and what the
nature of her relationship was to him.

And as she did,
it became clear how brutally she had
been wounded by him, both physically
and emotionally, in their relationship.

Everyone was shocked.
I was shocked.

And before I knew it,
there she was,
an 18-year-old college freshman
standing in front of 20 of her peers,
singing the intimate story of who she was.

Brené Brown
—in her now famous TED talk on vulnerability—
defined having courage as "telling the story of
who you are with your whole heart."

Her definition could not have been more fitting.

But it's worth taking a moment to ponder the fact
that what inspired this courage in my friend, was
none other than her attempt to empathize with
an other, namely Blanche.

The act of trying to empathize with an other,
inspired her to tell the story
of who she is.

Think about that for a second.

Can you think of any other times when an
attempt to empathize with an other actually
helped you tell your story?

I can.

That time I tried to write or present clearly
for others? It helped me better understand
and express my own thoughts.

That time I tried to empathize with my bipolar friend?
It helped me become more honest with myself.

That time I tried to empathize with how raw
materials worked? It helped me become better
at making things I wanted to make.

CHAPTER 5

Everything you do to empathize with an other, ultimately helps you empathize
with yourself.
The act of trying to empathize with an other turns out to be intrinsically reciprocal. And not in the sense of giving and receiving gifts or exchanging favors, but in the sense that the act of giving
is, in and of itself,
an act of receiving.

The nature of the act is neither selfish nor altruistic. It is simply a loop that cannot be untangled without losing its meaning.

This is the cardiac cycle
of any meaningful relationship.

And this can also be

a model
for design.

CHAPTER 5

[1] The part where various experts—be it designers, anthropologists, psychologists—go out in to the field to gain insights into people's constraints, needs, and motivations, in order to decide what to design and how.

When the word "empathy" is mentioned in the context of design, it is often misunderstood as being solely a part of user research.[1]

This is not the case.

Whatever phase of the design process you're in, or whatever method you're employing, for whatever purpose, there is always a potential to realize your empathy by engaging in an empathic conversation.

Starting out a project is an opportunity to engage in an empathic conversation with the various stakeholders.

Conducting interviews or observations in the field is an opportunity to engage in an empathic conversation with potential users.

Analyzing the results of user research is an opportunity to engage in an empathic conversation with teammates.

And even that's not all of it.

Prototyping with materials is an opportunity to engage in an empathic conversation with the materials.

Gauging how much impact a design has on the natural environment, is an opportunity to engage in an empathic conversation with the natural environment.

Reflecting on the progress of the project on your own is an opportunity to engage in an empathic conversation with yourself.

And so on and so forth.

The entire process of design *can be a multi-dimensional* empathic conversation.

There's a play I like called *The Real Thing*, where one of the characters talks about how in biblical Greek, "knowing" someone was a term for "making love."[2]

[2] The word is "yada."

He talks about the knowledge of each other
—not of the flesh but through the flesh—
knowledge of self, the real him, the real her, in
extremis the mask slipped from the face.

> It's to do with knowing and being known. I remember how it stopped seeming odd that in biblical Greek knowing was used for making love. Whosit knew so-and-so. Carnal knowledge. It's what lovers trust each other with. Knowledge of each other, not of the flesh but through the flesh, knowledge of self, the real him, the real her, in extremis, the mask slipped from the face.
> **HENRY / THE REAL THING**

What he's saying is that we cannot say that we know the other until we have tried to be sufficiently honest with ourselves, to have had the courage to feel naked in front of them, enough to have been able to elicit honesty from the other.

In the same way,
when design is framed as an empathic conversation, it is no longer just a way to produce products and services. Instead, it is a process **of coming to know and to trust the others** involved in the process.

> Philosophy is the wisdom of love at the service of love.
> **EMMANUEL LEVINAS / PHILOSOPHER**

This is not a process that ends when we ship our products and services. As a matter of fact, *it may never end.* This is not merely about fulfilling people's needs, either. It is also about coming to know who we are as human beings. It is to empower each and every one of us to tell the story of who we are. A story that can only be told by engaging in an empathic conversation with one other.

The ideas I have tried to share in this
book, is that to realize our empathy
is to make,
and to make
is to realize our empathy.
That it is a process through which we not only develop
our sensitivity, knowledge, and skill, but also identity.
That it is at the heart of what it means to be.

That it is a human right.

And we may never empathize with each other 100 percent,
just as we may never achieve absolute honesty.

But that's okay,
as long as the desire is there. As long as the conscious
effort to reach the goal is there. Because whether or not
we achieve this goal of realizing empathy, when we're
in pursuit of it,
all these wonderful things like innovation,
transformation, and collaboration emerge as
side effects and motivate us to keep trying.

> He who seeks truth shall find beauty. He who seeks beauty shall find vanity. He who seeks order shall find gratification. He who seeks gratification shall be disappointed. He who considers himself a servant of his fellow beings shall find the joy of self expression. He who seeks self expression shall fall into the pit of arrogance.
>
> **MOSHE SAFDIE / ARCHITECT**

CHAPTER 5

As far as I can tell, the continual development of computer technology is a given. The same holds true for the fact that it will continue to play a role in mediating the relationship between human beings.

The responsibility of those who have a deep enough understanding of both the current state of our abusive relationship to computer technology and the materiality of the computer itself, is to proactively devise courses of action aimed at changing the current state of our relationship to computer technology into preferred ones.

> Everyone designs who devises course of action aimed at changing existing situations into preferred ones.
> **HERBERT SIMON / ECONOMIST**

And what these past four years have made clear to me is what "preferred" means in this context. What I have realized is that "preferred" in this context is not about humanizing computer technology or being human-centric in its design. Instead, **it is to facilitate an empathic conversation** between the computer and us. And not because we need a better computer, the way we need a better mousetrap, but because we deserve to be in better relationships with whatever it is that we come to interact with.

But this does not mean we go around interfering with everyone's existing relationships with their computers. That could very well be considered non-empathic. Instead, what it means is to design so as to empower others to experience for themselves the value of being in a better relationship.

> To change something, build a new model that makes the existing model obsolete.
> **BUCKMINSTER FULLER / DESIGN SCIENTIST**

This is the ethics of design.

And by ethics, I don't mean the kind of ethics that preaches a moral and virtuous life, but rather the kind that aims to empower each and every one of us to experience for ourselves the value of engaging in their own acts of design, of making, of engaging in empathic conversations.

> The design arts are fundamentally a practical service to human beings in the accomplishment of individual and collective purposes. That is, the end purpose of design is to help other people accomplish their own purposes.
> **RICHARD BUCHANAN / PHILOSOPHER**

And not only that, but also to feel encouraged to continue, to sustain these conversations, to realize their empathy over time and memory, so as to be able to find their own meaning of making through their own making of meaning.

We often talk about technology as being an extension of ourselves. But rarely do we bother to delve into what that means.

When we consider something to be an extension of ourselves, it's because we're able to engage
in an empathic conversation with them.

It is the case when playing a musical instrument, driving an automobile, dancing with another person, or even dancing alone.

It is also through empathic conversations that we are able to learn not only who others are, but also who we are, and how we are related to each other.

And as we learn this, we connect with each other at levels never before thought possible, which inspires us to stay humble and courageous, to wake up the next morning curious to engage further.

What this ultimately gives us is a reason to keep living,
to sustain life.

As far as I can tell, this is what the art of making has been doing since the dawn of time.

Is this not the same purpose design aims to serve?

This is design not "for" others, but "with" others.

This is design not as a means to change others' behaviors, or to solve their problems, but to empower them to learn about themselves, others, and their relationships.

> In the seventies I reacted against design methods. I disliked the machine language, the behaviorism, the continual attempt to fix the whole of life into a logical framework... I realize now that rational and scientific knowledge is essential for discovering the bodily limits and abilities we all share, but that mental process, the mind, is destroyed if it is encased in a fixed frame of reference.
> J. CHRISTOPHER JONES / DESIGNER

This is design as an attitude of humility and courage, aspiring to give rise to our honesty, sincerity, integrity, and dignity.

This is design as a way of being in the world, at every moment, armed with the conscious effort to make our own meanings in our lives.

This is design as empathic conversation.

The child who transfers the word "mama" from all humans to all females and then to his mother is not just learning what "mama" means or who his mothers is. Simultaneously he is learning some of the differences between males and females as well as something about the ways in which all but one female will behave toward him. His reactions, expectations, and beliefs—indeed, **much of his perceived world—change** accordingly. By the same token, the Copernicans who denied its traditional title "planet" to the sun were not only learning what "planet" meant or what the sun was. Instead, they were changing the meaning of "planet" so that it could continue to make useful distinctions in a world where all celestial bodies, not just the sun, were seen differently from the way they had been seen before... Paradigms determine large areas of experience at the same time.

THOMAS KUHN / PHILOSOPHER

SLIM

If cubists took "perspective," which used to be a means to an end for renaissance artists (a poor way of putting it, I know, but I hope you understand what I mean) as the very content behind their work, then what I seem to desire is to take "physics," or more specifically how our relationships "work," which is a means to an end for those who make things in the physical world, as the very content behind my work. I never thought of it this way, but it seems to make sense.

The word "confidence" in Chinese characters as adopted by the Koreans is written as 自信感 (자신감), which is made up of the words "self," "trust," and "feeling." Isn't that beautiful?

As a matter of fact, every single Chinese character seems to be a piece of poem trying to capture some kind of quality seemingly impossible to capture in words. Take the word person (人) as an example. Just two strokes leaning against each other. Isn't that just beautiful? To be a person is not to be me, but we. Who were these people that invented this language? What were they thinking? All of a sudden, after all these years spending time studying and working in the U.S., I am all of a sudden seeing new things from the cultures of my past. How could I have been so blind?

281

December 7, 2009 12:33 p.m.

April 17, 2010 2:10 p.m.

EPILOGUE

On July 12 2011,

right after finishing the first draft of the book,
I had a chance to conduct another
interview with Dr. Lewis Lipsitt.

Towards the end of our interview, we somehow
digressed to talking about why some people are able
to lead fulfilling and satisfying lives despite hardship,
while others who enjoy abundance fail to do so. And
he said something quite remarkable.

He said that whether or not someone develops a strong
sense of trust in others and the world at large can have
a great deal of impact in deciding this factor.

I was puzzled.

What did such a broad sense of trust have
anything to do with living a fulfilling life?

But since the topic was a digression from our
original discussion, I left it at that, and returned
to the main thread.

On my return home, the idea kept bothering
me like an unscratchable itch.

What did trust in others and the world at large
have to do with leading a fulfilling life?

I suppose it would make a person nicer to be so
trusting of others, which can make them feel
good about themselves.

But what else?

Then I was reminded of a Korean saying that
I had frequently heard as a child: "믿음, 소망, 사랑
그중에 제일은 사랑이요," which roughly translates
to "trust, hope, love: greatest among them, love."
And with that, the relationship became clear.

If your experience is anything like mine,
life is filled with feelings of uncertainty.

But thankfully,
there are also moments when we feel a sense of
certainty. By and large, it is the oscillation between
the two feelings that not only keeps us sane, but also
creates the momentum of this pendulum called life.

Given what Dr. Lipsitt said about trust, I am
now compelled to qualify this feeling of certainty
as a manifestation of our trust in others and the
world at large.

In other words, instead of thinking about trust as
something we do or give, we can also think of it
as a sensation of certainty that we embody.

Music, for example, is one of my sources of trust.

When I feel betrayed and scarred by people, music
is something I can count on to be there for me when
I need it. When I am down, I can listen to my favorite
song and feel as if it is speaking to me. When I hear
a lyric that resonates, I can feel as though I am being
heard. When I am making music, I can feel both. But
most importantly, these feelings are consistent,
which means that I trust that my future interactions
with music will continue to afford the same qualities.

[When] I first meet my patients... they show clear signs of mistrust.
I personify everything unknown and foreign to them. However,
as the music unfolds, they often seem to experience a basic grain
of trust in the music itself, as if their mistrust gives way to the
qualities of "humanness" inherent in music. Through musical
activity, they can recognize humanity in another person, humanity
that extends beyond their culture and experience of trauma.

GARY ANSDELL / MUSIC THERAPIST

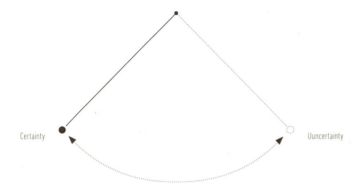

The computer is another source of my trust.

Perhaps this is an experience unique to hackers, but once I became sufficiently conversant with the computer using languages such as Assembly and C, I was not only able to specify what I wanted it to do, but also predict how it would behave in response to my requests. Not only that, but also what effect those behaviors would have on the computer itself. And once again, this happened consistently such that I can trust my future interactions with the computer will continue to afford the same qualities.

> Adam describes his creativity in Civilization as "just the right amount of creating. It's not like you really have to do something new. But it feels new... It's a very comforting kind of thing, this repetitive sort of thing, it's like, 'I'm building a city—oh, yes, I built a city.'" These are feelings of accomplishment on a time scale and with a certainty that the real cannot provide.
>
> SHERRY TURKLE / SOCIOLOGIST

As you can see, there can be many different sources
of trust. As a matter of fact, depending on your ability
to engage in empathic conversations, what you may
consider a subject of trust may be limitless.

Unfortunately, however, there is no denying the fact
that at any given moment, we cannot possibly fathom
the entirety of the other, let alone the world at large.
Therefore, even if we think we know the pattern that
governs an other's behavior, there may be a factor that we
are unaware of that can eventually break this pattern.

And when this unknown factor is introduced,
our interaction with these sources of trust may
no longer afford the qualities we expect it to.
        As it often does.
More so in our relationship to a human "other" than not.

The fact of the matter is,
we do not "know" things.

We trust that we know things.

I am wiser than this human being. For probably neither of us
knows anything noble and good, but he supposes he knows
something when he does not know, while I, just as I do not know,
do not even suppose that I do.

SOCRATES / PHILOSOPHER

When our sense of trust gets shaken,
so does our knowledge.

If this makes living sound risky,
that's because it is.
    And if you have ever felt hurt and betrayed
in the process, you understand what I mean.

But what may not be so obvious is that, feeling a sense of
certainty in relation to others and the world at large, is not
an exercise in trusting an other, but rather in trusting
your own incomplete understanding
of that other.

And of course the accuracy and precision of your
understanding of the other is directly proportional to
you ability to empathize with them.

As a matter of fact,
depending on how much significance you give to your
own understanding, the boundary between trust and
faith can become rather blurry.

But what remains is that if you would like to have your
moments of certainty, if you would like to maintain the
oscillation of life, you must be willing to trust something.
You simply have no choice, but to take the risk.

This is the very tension
of our vulnerable existence.
It is our very soul.

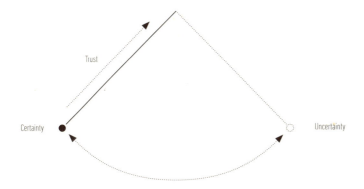

But trust alone is not enough, either.

Or more precisely,
    unilateral trust is not enough.

Because just as a pendulum loses its oscillation due to the resistance it experiences in the air, we lose our ability to trust by experiencing something we call *fear.*

So if we do not wish the oscillation to
die out because of our accrual of fear
—which is inevitable with painful experiences—
there must exist another force.

A force that attempts to ground us, gives us weight, and pulls us toward them without tying us down. A force that can aide in restoring a sense of balance to the system. The most powerful force known to mankind.

    The force of love.

Seen in this light, life is not a pursuit of reproduction, but reproduction is a means of bettering one's chances of giving, receiving, and perpetuating love.

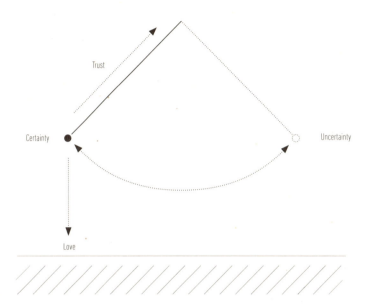

What's amazing about love is that even in the absence of a clear purpose or an objective, our love of each other can sustain our lives. And as it does, it can also give us hope. Hope of good things to come.

Why?

Because we've already experienced what love feels like. Who is to say that we won't get to feel more of it? Perhaps it's possible to feel something even better! Who knows? Why not stay alive to find out? Why not have hope?

Michael Shurtleff, one of the most preeminent
American casting directors of all time, says in his
landmark book *Audition,* that to act out a scene,
an actor must ask herself a simple question:

"What am I fighting for?"

In each of the scenes we act in this play called life,
we're fighting for love.
   Plain and simple.

We can either live accepting or die rejecting. And
accepting this idea would obviously make us
intensely vulnerable, as very few would publicly
announce their acceptance of such an idea.

But if there is anything I have learned in the past four
years, it is that an honest expression of the "self"
—the kind that constantly changes—
   is the only way to profound resonance. That there is
   every reason to believe that those who touch the hearts
   of millions are doing their very best to be honest with
   themselves even if they may never achieve it.

But let's not sugar-coat things here.
If you have ever tried to create a piece of artwork that
requires you to honestly express your "self," you know
how lonely it can feel, how scary and painful it can be.

As a matter of fact,
it took me all my life to come to the
realization that the absence of love
is death.

Because there is a distinct possibility that you may
get sufficiently hurt in this process that you will feel
that you cannot continue to trust.

This is what happens with people experiencing
severe depression. It is a helpless, hopeless feeling.
A feeling that you are completely and utterly alone.
And to make matters worse, it feels as though
there's absolutely nothing you can do about it.

It is devastating.

So devastating, in fact, taking your
own life seems like a logical choice.

As many do.

To be honest,
    this is not the kind of realization I was expecting to come to when I embarked on this journey through art school. If anything, I was naïvely expecting an answer to the age-old question:

"why am I here?"

    I thought I'd eventually arrive at some grand purpose, a grand cause to fight for the greater good of humanity: something to make my life seem amazing and worthwhile.

    After all, the motto I lived my twenties by was

"to change the world."

Clearly,
    my thirties should be guided by something even greater.

    But instead, what I ended up realizing was the intensely fragile nature of what it means to be
        a human being.

    What it means to trust,

to hope,

        to love.

Yet,

I feel relieved to know that there doesn't have to be an answer to the "why?" question. Because what Dr. Lipsitt taught me is that the function of that question is not to get an answer.

Instead,
it is to give anyone who dares to ask the question a deep sense of trust in ourselves that we can—and will—find an answer. It is what starts the cycle of trust, hope, and love. It is the first sign that you have made a conscious decision to care about your life, to promise to fight for love, to embrace what it means to be a human being.

That is what trust has to do with leading a fulfilling life.
Nothing more. Nothing less.

What we ultimately gain from making, from engaging in an empathic conversation, is not just a thing, or even the experience, but the ability to trust ourselves and others that make up the world at large.

It is the ability to love.

And with love, we bring into this world the necessary energy to sustain each other's lives, to give each other the means to wake up the next morning ready to make more.

And when what we make inspires others to engage in the kind of empathic conversation it took us to make, it can provide them with their own sources of trust.

As simple and as powerful as that can be,
that is the function of art.

So whatever it is you make,
whether a chair, a piece of software, a story, a service,
an organization, a building, a city, or a movement,

remember

that unless it becomes a source of your trust,
unless it activates your soul, unless it empowers
you to love, and find hope, unless it gives you
a reason to sustain your life, to live another day,
you have not yet finished your work.

So here's to finishing our work.

Stay beautiful.

Always. ■

I believe that love that is true and real
creates a respite from death.
All cowardice comes from not loving or not loving
well, which is the same thing. And when the man who
is brave and true looks death squarely in the face like
some rhino hunters I know or Belmonte, who is truly
brave, it is because they love with sufficient passion
to push death out of their minds...
until it returns, as it does, to all men... And then you must
make really good love again.
Think about it.

ERNST HEMMINGWAY / MIDNIGHT IN PARIS

SLIM   This is my second semester learning what it means to "dance." Or as I like to call it "make with our body." I have to say that I am getting a lot more than I bargained for. Last week our team did a site-specific improvisational performance piece, which taught me, in a visceral way, that in a truly collaborative team, there is no leader. No. Actually, that's not quite right. There is no one leader. There are leaders that take turns, but at each moment we're not fully cognizant of who that will be next.

Sitting in a post-mortem reflecting on how we came up with our performance, Jude, one of the team members, said that he felt like he was following the rest of the group. Well I felt like I was following the rest of the group, too! My guess is that we all felt that way at one point or another.

I also remember the feeling of fear and uneasiness I felt the first time we stumbled upon our site—a chemical storage room (no, it's not full of chemicals, but just a lot of metallic junk, and gas tanks and such). It didn't seem like the safest place to perform, but I think it was Hanne, the other team member, who just started climbing up on different platforms and junked shelves. I think it was that act that motivated me to let go of my own fear and see where this could take us. That kind of peer pressure or

March 10, 2011 8:03 p.m.

modeling can be a nice way to get out of our comfort zone (of course, not all peer pressure is created equal).

What this tells me is that I've misunderstood what it means to improvise. To improvise is not to be arbitrary. It is to retain the individual integrity and perspective, but to allow the relationship of those individuals to bring that integrity and perspective into a proportion that creates a beautiful whole. I suppose I've known all this theoretically, and I've been in collaborative situations, not to mention successful ones, but to feel this now at this level of physicality seems to be a whole different kind of thing. Such a simple idea, yet so profound. Not to mention difficult to achieve.

AFTERWORD

DAVID

Computers are a real problem.

The previous assertion is manifestly unfair. Computers are what they are, and too often we reify them and let them be scapegoats for all the frustrations we have with them, all of the unmet expectations we have for them, and all of the pain we experience from our interactions with them.

Our malaise begins with confusion. We say "computer" but we do not make clear whether we are referring to the physical thing, the aspects of that thing we interact with (keyboard, mouse, and screen), the software that makes the thing what it appears to be at any moment in time, or the fit/misfit between the thing and its context. Ignorance amplifies our discontent.

As Seung Chan points out early in his book, computers have materiality—they are something, something physical, something with their own "physics." We do not see this reality and so we misunderstand and misunderstanding leads to anger. Fatalism stops us from trying to do anything different. We sincerely believe, "that's just the way it is"; "the computer won't let me"; even absurdities like, "I can't help you, the computer says you died last year."

AFTERWORD

The "we" in the preceding paragraphs is the public that is increasingly unhappy with computers and the world that seem to be shaping around us. What of the professionals, the computer scientists, the software engineers, and the interaction designers? Unfortunately, they are just as sloppy in their use of language and imprecise about what a computer is as are everyone else; and, they too often suffer from the ignorance, the lack of understanding of "materialness." Professionals do, however, seem to believe that things can be different, that there is a better way and perhaps that way is grounded in the notion of design.

In this book, Seung Chan provides us with a personal narrative, a recounting of an exploration into art and making and how this changed his understanding of what design might be, and why the change is essential. Seung Chan takes us to a very different territory and a very different understanding of what design is and might be than that shared by most computer professionals. To see how different it is, it is useful to revisit some professional history.

In the 1980s, I taught my first university class in computer science called "Systems Analysis and Design." The title of the class is misleading. Two of the terms—systems and design—had so little content behind them they were essentially not addressed. The core of the class was techniques for extracting a precise definition of all the data elements and all of the transformation algorithms necessary to satisfy a set of requirements. System meant only the program or a set of programs. The only thing "designed" was the program—the arrangement of a set of "black boxes" with defined data coming in one side and transformed data leaving the other. There was but one arrangement—or architecture—appropriate for connecting these black boxes: hierarchical command and control.

What was to be learned in the class was how to build an artifact, a thing analogous to a building or a bridge. The artifact was the system: the girders, the cables, the paint, the bolts. Sometimes the boundaries of the system were extended. The system that was a bridge might include that which used the bridge; the system that was a building might include the people in that building. But in both cases the only thing of interest about vehicles or people was their mass and volume and number, and maybe patterns or frequencies of encounters with them.

The inspiration and initial justification for the "artifact fetish" of software engineering was an architect, a designer of buildings and cities. When the software and computer community came together in 1968 to create the discipline

DAVID

AFTERWORD

and practice called "software engineering," one of the most cited and influential sources of ideas was a book by Christopher Alexander titled, *Notes on the Synthesis of Form*. Alexander's intent was to create a "science of design" grounded in a calculus of sorts—mathematical formulas that would yield optimal solutions (designs) for any combination of variables and constraints (he called these forces). A "science of software" was precisely the object of the experts and industry leaders gathered at the NATO conference in 1968.

A superficial reading of the first pages of Seung Chan's work might seem to reflect a similar focus on the artifact. Speaking of the importance of understanding "materiality" and analogies with furniture or talking of the arrangement of ones and zeros to create a computer program might distract one into thoughts of artifacts. Even the empathic conversation between the craftsman and that which is crafted can feel a bit artifact-centric. This is not his intent; it is but a starting point for understanding something of much greater scope and something far more profound.

A hint as to the destination Seung Chan is leading us to can be seen in the contrast of ideas put forth by Fred Brooks and Peter Naur. Fred Brooks wrote one of the most cited papers in software, "No Silver Bullet," discussing the difficulty of developing software. He classified all the problems and issues into "accidental" and "essential." Accidental problems could be solved with advances in technique and technology, but essential problems were simply hard. Chief among these was the "conceptual construct," a mental model of executing software.

Brooks believed that the complexity of the conceptual construct was beyond normal human capabilities. For this and a few other reasons he concluded that the ultimate solution to the software design problem was better designers. Thirty or so years later Brooks wrote, *The Design of Design*, a compilation of his thoughts about how one might create and nurture great designers. Design is still nothing more than decisions made about the artifact—the program —and how to improve the conceptual constructs that determined the form and execution of the program.

Peter Naur was also concerned with mental models, which he called "theories." A theory is a mental model of "an affair of the world and how the software might handle and support it." But the focus of a theory is not the artifact but the whole system in which the artifact is but another actor. Theories, for Naur, come into existence via conversations among

AFTERWORD

communities of humans playing various roles: from user, to owner, to manager, to developer, to tester. But the conversation also includes artifacts, abstract models, executing programs. (Richard Gabriel's essay, "The Designed as Designer," illuminates how conversations with the inanimate and abstract occur.)

My first read of *Realizing Empathy* focused on literal understanding with the occasional spice that comes from recognizing echoes of my own thoughts and those of other authors whom I admire. The second reading was an attempt to engage in an empathic conversation with the work, and through it with the author. The third read felt very much like an empathic conversations with the author, with Dahl and Nygaard (Simula), with Pelle Ehn, with Kay and Ingalls (Smalltalk), with Maturana and Varela, with Peter Naur, and even Hui Neng (Sixth Patriarch of Zen).

Each successive reading reinforced the conviction that the observations and insights gained by Seung Chan in his personal journey are both profound and profoundly true. The principles he advances form a foundation for understanding design, but not the design of artifacts (although they apply to artifact design), not the design of systems or processes (although they apply equally well to those things), but to the design of reality.

For a couple of decades now, I have been arguing that what we are engaged in as software professionals is reality construction—literally altering the way that people work, live, love, play, think, and feel. What I did not consciously recognize, until I read *Realizing Empathy,* was the inherent dualism in my thinking about reality. Reality was just a great big complex artifact, from which I, as designer, was separate. Seung Chan's elaboration of the principle of empathic conversation eliminated that dualism for me. It obliterated the subject-object, actor-acted upon, separation implicit in the vocabulary of design and of software development.

Non-dualism is, in my opinion the most important understanding in *Realizing Empathy.* Which leads me to a final observation. Seung Chan concludes his work with the following paragraphs:

> *Whatever it is you make, whether a chair, a piece of software, a story, a service, an organization, a building, a city, or a movement, please remember that unless it becomes a source of your trust, unless it empowers you to love, find hope, and keep faith, unless it gives you a reason to sustain your life, to live another day, to stay curious enough to develop the humility and courage necessary to be honest with yourself, to empathize with*

AFTERWORD

others, unless it activates your soul, you have not yet finished your work.

Here's to finishing our work.

I would respectfully suggest that although our ephemeral focus might be on making a "chair, a piece of software, a story," we are actually engaged in (re)designing our collective reality which is ourselves. Until the Universe collapses upon itself to once again become a Singularity or achieves the ultimate order of absolute entropy.

Our work is ever unfinished.

    David West[1]
    February 9, 2013

[1] David West is coach and mentor serving organizations seeking system change for innovation, sustainability, and adaptability; and individuals engaged in the process of achieving mastery of software-driven systems design. He is the author of *Object Thinking*, and of numerous papers in the areas of objects, agile, and design. He is engaged in redefining/reinventing both a profession and the educational support required for that profession.

CONVERSATIONS

SLIM From February 25, 2011 to May 28, 2011, I set up a private blog, where I regularly engaged in conversations with five generous friends. I would post a piece of writing on the blog, they would comment on it, then based on the feedback, I would not only revise the writing, but also feel encouraged and inspired to keep writing. What came out of that process was the first draft of the book you are holding now. While much has changed since then, with their permission, I would love to share an edited version of those conversations with you.

To keep the heft of printed matter to a manageable amount, the conversations have been made available in digital format. To access the conversations, please visit http://realizingempathy.com/

323

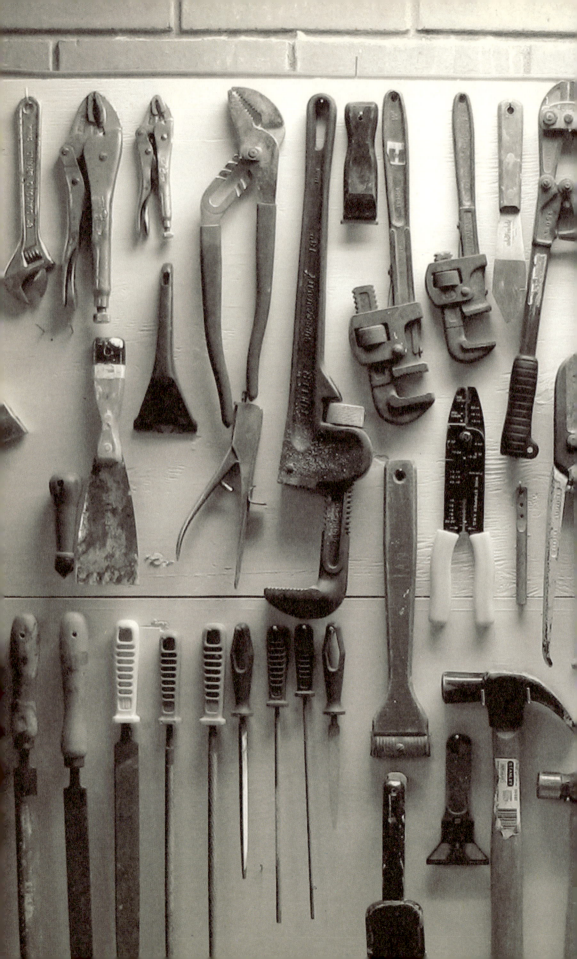

BIBLIOGRAPHY

Here are the citations for the quotes, notes, and photographs.

Dedication

Quotes

page xxiii   Pausch, Randy, and Jeffrey Zaslow. *The Last Lecture.*
New York: Hyperion, 2008. 121–122.

Notes

page xvii   The Last Lecture. "The Last Lecture | Randy Pausch."
Last modified March, 2008. http://thelastlecture.com.

page xix   Klug, Chris and Jesse Schell. "Syllabus (2012 Fall) | Building Virtual Worlds."
Last modified July 25, 2009. http://bvw.etc.cmu.edu/content/syllabus.

Photographs

page xiii   Robins, Gabriel, photographer. Dr. Randy Pausch at University of Virginia giving a talk on "Time Management." Photograph. Charlottesville, VA.
http://www.cs.virginia.edu/~robins/Randy/Randy_TM_jow0177.jpg.

page xxv   Lim, Seung Chan, photographer. "Acting exercise in Introduction to Acting and Directing at Brown University." Photograph. Providence, RI.

Preface
Quotes

Markoff, John. *What the Dormouse Said: How the Sixties Counterculture Shaped the Personal Computer Industry.* New York: Viking, 2005. 70. — *page xlvi*

Levy, Steven. *Hackers.* Sebastopol, CA: O'Reilly Media, 2010. 364. — *page xlvii*

Kawae, Yuki. E-mail message to the RISD community, December 13, 2012. — *page lii*

Bois, W.E.B. *The Social Theory of W.E.B. Du Bois.* Edited by Phil Zuckerman. Thousand Oaks: Pine Forge Press, 2004. 206. — *page lv*

Weizenbaum, Joseph. *Computer Power and Human Reason: From Judgment to Calculation.* San Francisco: W.H. Freeman, 1976. 236. — *page lxi*

Notes

Crawford, Matthew B. *Shop Class as Soulcraft: An Inquiry into the Value of Work.* New York: Penguin Books, 2010. — *page xli*

Hasbrouck, Edward. "Peacework Back Issues | Life Outside the Mainframe: August 2005." Accessed February 7, 2013. http://www.peaceworkmagazine.org/pwork/0508/050814.htm. — *page xlv*

Photographs

Wang, Jiuguang, photographer. "Hammerschlag Hall at Carnegie Mellon University" Photograph. Pittsburgh, PA. http://www.flickr.com/photos/jiuguangw/5134927859/sizes/o/ — *page xxxi*

Unknown photographer. "Using the Portable Bandsaw in Metal Casting at the Rhode Island School of Design." Photograph. Providence, RI. — *page 1*

Introduction
Quotes

page 9   Dreyfuss, Henry. *Designing for People*. New York: Allworth Press, 2003. 24.

page 13   Lucas, Peter, Joe Ballay, and Mickey McManus. *Trillions: Thriving in the Emerging Information Ecology*. Hoboken, NJ.: Wiley, 2012. 2.

page 14   Wilson, Cody. "The Wiki Weapon - YouTube." Accessed February 7, 2013. http://www.youtube.com/watch?v=AQ6Q3BfbVBU.

page 17   Hamming, Richard. "You and Your Research." Accessed February 7, 2013. http://www.cs.virginia.edu/~robins/YouAndYourResearch.html.

Notes

page 13   Black, Richard. "BBC News - Species Count Put at 8.7 Million." Accessed February 7, 2013. http://www.bbc.co.uk/news/science-environment-14616161.

Photographs

page 5   Lim, Seung Chan, photographer. "Charcoal Figure Drawings in Freshmen Drawing Foundations at the Rhode Island School of Design." Photograph. Providence, RI.

page 19   Lim, Seung Chan, photographer. "Bank of Lathes in the Industrial Design Metal Shop at the Rhode Island School of Design." Photograph. Providence, RI.

Prologue
Quotes

page 37   Proust, Marcel, and Charles Kenneth Moncrieff. *The Captive; The Fugitive; Time Regained*. New York: Vintage Books, 1982. 932.

Notes

page 27   Encyclopædia Britannica Online, s. v. "Bipolar Disorder," accessed February 5, 2013, http://www.britannica.com/EBchecked/topic/362153/bipolar-disorder.

Photograph

Lim, Seung Chan, photographer. "*The Woods* as Performed by Alex Ashe and Lizzie Stanton in Acting I at Brown University." Photograph. Providence, RI. *page 23*

Interview

Quotes

Rifkin, Jeremy. *The Empathic Civilization: The Race to Global Consciousness in a World in Crisis*. New York: J.P. Tarcher/Penguin, 2009. 155. *page 67*

Notes

Bretherton, Inge. "The Origins of Attachment Theory: John Bowlby and Mary Ainsworth." *Developmental Psychology* 28 (1992): 759–775. *page 41*

Hazan, Cindy, and Phillip R. Shaver. "Romantic Love Conceptualized as an Attachment Process." *Journal of Personality and Social Psychology* 52 (1987): 511–24. *page 41*

Rizzolatti, Giacomo, and Laila Craighero. "The Mirror-Neuron System." *Annual Review of Neuroscience* 27 (2004): 169–192. *page 45*

Di Pellegrino, G., L. Fadiga, L. Fogassi, V. Gallese, and G. Rizzolatti. "Understanding Motor Events: A Neurophysiological Study." *Experimental Brain Research* 91 (1992): 176–180. *page 45*

Encyclopædia Britannica Online, s. v. "Conditioning," accessed December 28, 2012, http://www.britannica.com/EBchecked/topic/131552/conditioning. *page 45*

Encyclopædia Britannica Online, s. v. "Conditioning," accessed December 28, 2012, http://www.britannica.com/EBchecked/topic/131552/conditioning. *page 45*

A.D.A.M. Medical Encyclopedia [Internet]. Atlanta (GA): A.D.A.M., Inc.; 1997-2012. Sudden Infant Death Syndrome; [last updated 2011 Aug 02; cited 2012 Dec 28]; Available from: http://www.nlm.nih.gov/medlineplus/ency/article/001566.htm *page 51*

Encyclopædia Britannica Online, s. v. "Human Nervous System," accessed December 28, 2012, http://www.britannica.com/EBchecked/topic/409709/human-nervous-system. *page 53*

page 60   Zamanian, Kaveh. "Attachment Theory as Defense: What Happened to Infantile Sexuality?" *Psychoanalytic Psychology* 28 (2011): 33–47.

page 61   Lawrence, Douglas H. "Acquired Distinctiveness of Cues: II. Selective Association in A Constant Stimulus Situation." *Journal of Experimental Psychology* 40(1950): 175–188.

Photographs

page 65   Lim, Seung Chan, photographer. "Dr. Lewis Lipsitt." Photograph. Providence, RI.

page 69   Bee, Jude, photographer. "Improvised Dance Performance by Annie Rose London, Sofia Unanue, and Seung Chan Lim in Intermediate Modern Dance at Brown University." Photograph. Providence, RI.

Empathy
Quotes

page 75   Fry, Douglas. *Beyond War : The Human Potential for Peace*. Oxford New York: Oxford, 2007. xiv.

page 76   Lorenz, Konrad. *On Aggression*. New York: Harcourt Brace Jovanovich, 1974. 237.

page 77   de Waal, Frans. *The Age of Empathy: Nature's Lessons for A Kinder Society*. New York: Harmony Books, 2009. 10.

page 79   Lakoff, George, and Mark Johnson. *Metaphors We Live By*. Chicago: University of Chicago Press, 2003. 3.

page 80   Csikszentmihalyi, Mihaly. *Flow: The Psychology of Optimal Experience*. New York: Harper & Row, 1990. 105.

page 80   Ibid. 71.

page 80   Kohut, Heinz. "Introspection, Empathy, and Psychoanalysis; an Examination of the Relationship Between Mode of Observation and Theory." *Journal of the American Psychoanalytic Association* Jul, vol. 7, no. 3. (1959): 459-83. 459. doi: 10.1177/000306515900700304.

page 81   Fosshage, James. "Self psychology: The Self and Its Vicissitudes Within a Relational Matrix." In *Relational Perspectives in Psychoanalysis*. Edited by Neil Skolnick, and Susan C. Warshaw. Hillsdale, NJ: Analytic Press, 1992, 21–42. 23.

page 81   Selzer, Richard. *The Exact Location of the Soul: New and Selected Essays*. New York: Picador USA, 200. 30.

page 82   Chase, Stuart. *The Tyranny of Words*. New York: Harcourt, Brace, 1966. 14.

page 85   Lakoff, George. "Contemporary Theory of Metaphor." In *Metaphor and Thought*. Edited by Andrew Ortony. Cambridge: Cambridge University Press, 1979. 202–203.

Notes

Shallit, Jeffrey. "Science, Pseudoscience, and the Three Stages of Truth." Department of Computer Science, University of Waterloo, 2005. 3. *page 76*

Batson, Daniel. "These Things Called Empathy: Eight Related But Distinct Phenomena." In *The Social Neuroscience of Empathy*. Edited by Jean Decety and William John Ickes. Cambridge, MA: MIT Press, 2009. 3–15. 4. *page 77*

Bateson, Gregory. *Steps to an Ecology of Mind*. New York: Ballantine, 1972. *page 79*

Varela, Francisco. *The Embodied Mind: Cognitive Science and Human Experience*. Cambridge, MA: MIT Press, 1991. *page 79*

Lakoff, George. *Philosophy in the Flesh: The Embodied Mind and Its Challenge to Western Thought*. New York: Basic Books, 1999. *page 79*

Titchener, Edward B. *Lectures of the Experimental Psychology of Thought Processes*, New York, Macmillian, 1909. *page 81*

Hoffman, Martin L. "Perspectives on The Difference Between Understanding People and Understanding Things: The Role of Affect." In *Social Cognitive Development: Frontiers and Possible Futures*. Edited by John H. Flavell and Lee Ross. Cambridge: Cambridge University Press, 1981. 67–81. *page 81*

Photographs

Lim, Seung Chan, photographer. "A Bridgeport in the Industrial Design Metal Shop at the Rhode Island School of Design." Photograph. Providence, RI. *page 71*

Lim, Seung Chan, photographer. "Pouring Molten Brass in Metal Casting at the Rhode Island School of Design." Photograph. Providence, RI. *page 87*

Realizing Empathy
Quotes

de Waal, Frans. *The Age of Empathy: Nature's Lessons for a Kinder Society*. New York: Harmony Books, 2009. 48. *page 97*

Rothschild, Babette, and Marjorie L. Rand. *Help for the Helper: the Psychophysiology of Compassion Fatigue and Vicarious Trauma*. New York: W.W. Norton, 2006. 47. *page 100*

Koestler, Arthur. *The Act of Creation*. London: Arkana [The Penguin Group], 1989. 647. *page 101*

Wu, Kuang-Ming. *On Metaphoring: A Cultural Hermeneutic*. Leiden: Brill, 2001. 399. *page 103*

Olin, Doris. *Paradox*. Montreal: McGill-Queen's University Press, 2003. 1. *page 103*

page 104	Festinger, Leon. *A Theory of Cognitive Dissonance*. Stanford, Calif.: Stanford University Press, 1962. 3.
page 104	Brown, Brené. "Brené Brown: The Power of Vulnerability - YouTube." YouTube. Accessed February 7, 2013. http://www.youtube.com/watch?v=iCvmsMzlF7o
page 106	Koestler, Arthur. *The Act of Creation*. London: Arkana [The Penguin Group], 1989. 35.
page 106	Please refer to page 59 of this book.
page 113	Bohm, David. *On Dialogue*. Edited by Lee Nichol. [Routlege classics ed. London: Routledge, 2004. 2.

Notes

page 90	Encyclopædia Britannica Online, s. v. "Lost-Wax Process," accessed February 05, 2013, http://www.britannica.com/EBchecked/topic/348436/lost-wax-process.
page 101	"What is Conversation? How Can We Design for Effective Conversation?" Accessed December 28, 2012. http://www.dubberly.com/articles/what-is-conversation.html.
page 104	"Consonance, n.". OED Online. December 2012. Oxford University Press. Accessed January 4, 2013. http://www.oed.com/view/Entry/39704.

Photographs

page 93	Lim, Seung Chan, photographer. "Demonstration of Traditional Malian Dance by Assi Coulibaly in Contemporary Mandé Performance at Brown University." Photograph. Providence, RI.
page 115	Kim, Yong Joo. "Using the Japanese Saw at Keeseh Studio." Photograph. Providence, RI.

Making and Empathy
Quotes

page 132	Sennett, Richard. *Respect in a World of Inequality*. New York: W.W. Norton, 200. 44
page 139	Brenda Ueland "The Art of Listening" San Jose Mercury News, October 25, 1992.
page 142	Saussure, Ferdinand. "Linguistic Value." In *The Routledge Language and Cultural Theory Reader*. Edited by Lucy Burke, Tony Crowley, and Alan Girvin. London: Routledge, 2000. 105–113. 111.
page 142	Stapleton, Laura. "Toward Present Listening: Practices and Verbal Response Patterns in Small Groups of Teacher Candidates and University Supervisors." Ph.D. diss., Stanford University, 2008. 33.

PBS. "Beat of a Different Drummer | PBS News Hour | June 14, 1999 | PBS."   *page 144*
PBS: Public Broadcasting Service. Accessed February 7, 2013.
http://www.pbs.org/newshour/bb/entertainment/jan-june99/
drummer_6-14.html.

Johns, H.D. *Serendipity: Discoveries Made While Doing Psychotherapy.*   *page 145*
Victoria, B.C.: Trafford, 2005. 193.

Gibson, James. "Constancy and Invariance in Perception"   *page 152*
In *The Nature and Art of Motion.* Edited by György Kepes. 60–70. 60.

Gowing, Lawrence. "The Logic of Organized Sensations."   *page 156*
In *Conversations with Cézanne,* edited by Michael Doran.
Berkeley: University of California Press, 2001. 180–212. 198.

Hagen, Uta. *A Challenge for the Actor.* New York: Scribner's; 1991. 53.   *page 167*

Gray, Henry D. "The First Quarto of *Hamlet*" *The Modern*   *page 167*
Language Review. Vol. 10, No. 2 (Apr., 1915), 171–180. 173.

Shakespeare, William. *As You Like It.* [Large print.] ed. Hollywood: *page 168*
Simon & Brown, 2011. 145.

Meisner, Sanford, and Dennis Longwell. *Sanford Meisner on Acting.*   *page 170*
New York: Vintage Books, 1987. 16.

Wu, Kuang-Ming. *On Metaphoring: A Cultural Hermeneutic.*   *page 175*
Leiden: Brill, 2001. 202.

Jones, J. Christopher. *Essays in Design.* Chichester   *page 191*
West Sussex: Wiley, 1984. 19-20.

Fortun, Michael, and Herbert J. Bernstein. *Muddling Through:*   *page 193*
Pursuing Science and Truths in the 21st Century.
Washington, D.C.: Counterpoint, 1998. 176.

Gantt, Horsely. "On humility in Science" *Integrative Physiological and*   *page 209*
Behavioral Science. October–December 1991, Volume 26,
Issue 4, 335-338. 335.

Notes

Encyclopædia Britannica Online, s. v. "Richard Serra," accessed   *page 129*
January 11, 2013, http://www.britannica.com/EBchecked/topic
/1093333/Richard-Serra.

Encyclopædia Britannica Online, s. v. "A Streetcar Named Desire,"   *page 163*
accessed January 15, 2013, http://www.britannica.com
/EBchecked/topic/568739/A-Streetcar-Named-Desire.

Bloom, Harold. *Shakespeare: The Invention of the Human.*   *page 166*
New York: Riverhead Books, 1998.

Hovanesian, Leon P. "About Those 3 Drawings..." Last mofidified March 16,   *page 190*
2009. http://welcome.risd.edu/2009/03/16/about-those-3-drawings/.

page 190   RISD. "Division of Foundation Studies." Accessed February 12, 2013. http://www.risd.edu/Academics/Foundation_Studies/.

Photographs

page 119   "Lim, Seung Chan, photographer. "Review of Paper-Folded Objects in Freshmen 3D Foundations at the Rhode Island School of Design." Photograph. Providence, RI."

page 211   Lim, Seung Chan, designer. "'Type in Space' poster designed completed in Type II at Rhode Island School of Design." Photograph. Providence, RI.

page 215   Lim, Seung Chan, photographer. "in the Hot Shop at the Rhode Island School of Design" Photograph. Providence, RI.

Facilitating Empathy
Quotes

page 224   Merleau-Ponty, Maurice. *Phenomenology of Perception: An Introduction.* London: Routledge, 2002. 171.

page 224   Bachelard, Gaston. *The Poetics of Space.* Boston: Beacon Press, 1994. 47.

page 225   Curry, Patrick. *Defending Middle-Earth: Tolkien, Myth and Modernity.* Boston: Houghton Mifflin, 2004. 49.

page 225   Merleau-Ponty, Maurice. *Phenomenology of Perception: An Introduction.* London: Routledge, 2002. 258.

page 226   van Tilburg, Miranda A.L. *Psychological Aspects of Geographical Moves Homesickness and Acculturation Stress.* Amsterdam: Amsterdam University Press, 2005. 39.

page 226   Jamieson, Lynn. *Intimacy: Personal Relationships in Modern Societies.* Cambridge: Polity, 1998. 9.

page 228   Isaacson, Walter. *Steve Jobs.* New York: Simon & Schuster, 2011. 129.

page 229   Esther Perel. "Esther Perel: The secret to desire in a long-term relationship - YouTube." Accessed February 15, 2013. http://www.ted.com/talks/esther_perel_the_secret_to_desire_in_a_long_term_relationship.html

page 234   Kant, Immanuel. *Lectures on Ethics.* Edited by J.B. Schneewind. Translated by Peter Lauchlan Heath. New York: Cambridge University Press, 1997. 231.

page 235   Ploeg, Jan Douwe van der. *The New Peasantries Struggles for Autonomy and Sustainability in an Era of Empire and Globalization.* London: Earthscan, 2008. 118.

page 236   Jenkins, Richard. *Social Identity.* 3rd ed. London: Routledge, 2008. 102–103.

page 236   Turkle, Sherry. *Evocative Objects: Things We Think With.* Cambridge, Ma.: MIT Press, 2007. 10.

Moss, Larry. *The Intent to Live: Achieving Your True Potential as an Actor.* *page 237*
Bantam trade pbk. ed. New York: Bantam Books, 2005. 226.

Cornell, Drucilla. *Between Women and Generations: Legacies of Dignity.* *page 237*
Lanham, Maryland: Rowman & Littlefield Publishers, 2005. 93.

Csikszentmihalyi, Mihaly. *Flow: The Psychology of Optimal* *page 240*
Experience. New York: Harper & Row, 1990. 64.

Erikson, Kai. "Notes on Trauma and Community." In *Trauma: Explorations* *page 241*
in Memory. Edited by Caruth, Cathy. Baltimore:
Johns Hopkins University Press, 1995. 183-199. 197-198.

Bohm, David. *On Dialogue.* Edited by Lee Nichol. *page 242*
Routlege Classics Ed. London: Routledge, 2004. 2.

Hall, Peter. "Structuring Symbolic Interaction: Communication and Power." *page 243*
In *Communication yearbook 4.* Edited by Dan Nimmo.
New Brunswick, N.J.: Transaction Books, 1980. 49-60. 58.

Wu, Kuang-Ming. *On Metaphoring: A Cultural Hermeneutic.* *page 246*
Leiden: Brill, 2001. 67.

Csikszentmihalyi, Mihaly. *Flow: The Psychology of Optimal Experience.* *page 247*
New York: Harper & Row, 1990, 59-60.

Turkle, Sherry. "Computational Reticence Why Women Fear the Intimate *page 251*
Machine." In *Technology and Women's Voices: Keeping in Touch.* Edited by
Cheris Kramarae. New York: Routledge & Kegan Paul, 1988. 41–61. 50.

Notes

Irwin D. Greenwald and Maureen Kane. 1959. "The Share 709 System: *page 245*
Programming and Modification." Journal of ACM 6, 2 (April 1959), 128-133.
doi: 10.1145/320964.320967.

Photographs

Lim, Seung Chan, photographer. "Acting Exercise with Director John Emigh *page 219*
and the Cast of 'A Perfect Wedding' in Leeds Theatre at Brown University."
Photograph. Providence, RI.

Unknown photographer. "Using the Letterpress in the Type Shop at the Rhode *page 253*
Island School of Design." Photograph. Providence, RI.

Lim, Seung Chan, photographer. "A Computer modeled after the form *page 257*
and scale of both a drafting table and a standing mirror."
Photograph. Providence, RI.

Design and Empathy
Quotes

Stoppard, Tom. *The Real Thing: A Play.* Boston: Faber & Faber, 1984. 62. *page 269*

page 269   Lévinas, Emmanuel. *Otherwise Than Being: Or, Beyond Essence.* Translated by Alphonso Lingis. Hague: M. Nijhoff; 1981. 162.

page 271   Safdie, Moshe, and John Kettle. *Form and Purpose.* Boston: Houghton Mifflin, 1982. 138.

page 272   Simon, Herbert A. *The Sciences of the Artificial.* 3rd ed. Cambridge, Mass.: MIT Press, 1996. 111.

page 273   Sieden, Lloyd Steven. *A Fuller View: Buckminster Fuller's Vision of Hope and Abundance for All.* Studio City, CA: Divine Arts, 2012. 236.

page 273   Buchanan, Richard. "Design Ethics." In *Encyclopedia of Science, Technology, and Ethics.* 504–510. 507.

page 275   Jones, J. Christopher. *Essays in Design.* Chichester West Sussex: Wiley, 1984. 22.

page 277   Kuhn, Thomas. *The Structure of Scientific Revolutions.* 3rd ed. Chicago: The University of Chicago Press, 1996. 128–129.

Photographs

page 261   Lim, Seung Chan, photographer. "Industrial Design Metal Shop at the Rhode Island School of Design." Photograph. Providence, RI.

page 279   Lim, Seung Chan, photographer. "Acting Exercise with Director Constance Crawford in the Introduction to Acting and Directing at Brown University." Photograph. Providence, RI.

Epilogue
Quotes

page 288   Pavlicevic, Mercedes and Gary Ansdell. *Community Music Therapy.* London: J. Kingsley Publishers, 2004. 241.

page 289   Turkle, Sherry. *Alone Together: Why We Expect More from Technology and Less from Each Other.* New York: Basic Books, 2012. 224.

page 290   Leibowitz, David. *The Ironic Defense of Socrates Plato's Apology.* Cambridge: Cambridge University Press, 2010. 75.

page 301   *Midnight in Paris.* DVD. Directed by Woody Allen. 2011. Sony Pictures Home Entertainment, 2011.

Photographs

page 283   Lim, Seung Chan, photographer, "Working with Aluminum in the Industrial Design Metal Shop at the Rhode Island School of Design." Photograph. Providence, RI.

page 303   Lim, Seung Chan. "Warming Up with Floor Exercises in the Beginning Modern Dance at Brown University." Photograph. Providence, RI.

Lim, Seung Chan, photographer. "Collection of paper folded objects in Freshmen 3D Foundations at the Rhode Island School of Design." Photograph. Providence, RI. *page 309*

Bibliography
Quotes

Wu, Kuang-Ming. *On Metaphoring: A Cultural Hermeneutic.* Leiden: Brill, 2001. 231. *page 341*

Photographs

Lim, Seung Chan, photographer "Graciela Kincade, Sam Jambrović, and others warming up in Cunningham Dance at Brown University." Photograph. Providence, RI. *page 321*

Ogilvie, Huw, photographer. "The Garage." Photograph. Canberra, Australia. http://www.flickr.com/photos/barto/28135419/sizes/o/. *page 325*

Kim, Yong Joo. "Lumber in the Woodshop." Photograph. Providence, RI. *page 343*

Kim, Yong Joo. "Seung Chan Lim." Photograph. Providence, RI. *page 353*

Interestingly, "interface" is a word in mechanics. Watches and computers are nothing until interfaced with humans. We interface with machines, which thereby interface among themselves. Machine-interfacing is metaphored from human-interfacing, which we are. That **we are by nature interfacing** means that we are constituted by interacting with the other, i.e., constituted by the other.

Interfacing is inter-constituting. Here "inter-" describes a two-way metaphorical traffic, to describe the operation of this two-way constitution. To put it in terms of knowledge, our constitutive interfacing bespeaks the fact **that our self-knowledge comes from the other,** our Socratic midwife. Since our life is not worth living, not human, without this self-knowledge that is other-evoked and other-constituted, this interfacial knowledge constitutes the very humanness of the person.

Such ontological knowledge is inter-constitutively metaphorical in that other-look ferries my face to me, myself to me.

KUANG-MING WU / HERMENEUT

SPECIAL NOTE

SLIM On February 1, 2012, I launched a Kickstarter project to raise the funds to self-publish this book. By March 12, 2012, thanks to the 364 backers who have shown their generous support to the project, we were able to raise a total of $34,780. I just wanted to take this opportunity to say "thank you" to all of you.

AT THE PLEDGE LEVEL OF $3,300 OR MORE: I would like to thank SeungHyun Lee, Young Hee Moon, and Young Ran Lim.

AT THE PLEDGE LEVEL OF $780 OR MORE: I would like to thank the Hsu family and Anna Lee.

AT THE PLEDGE LEVEL OF $275 OR MORE: I would like to thank Allen & Rebecca Wirfs-Brock, Anson Ann, Darren Chan, Hongki Kim, Leahmarie Gottlieb, Mathhilde Pignol, and Mickey McManus.

AT THE PLEDGE LEVEL OF $100 OR MORE: I would like to thank Anne M. Berg, Belinda Madrid, Brendan Griffin O'Neill, Bruce EungJe Lee, Cathy Oh, Christian Bellofatto, Christine Kofman, Christl Kagiyama, Connie Chun, Connor Scheu, David Watson, Debbie Miller, Donna Powers, Eray Chou, Erica Sloan, EunJee Kim,

345

GrafikSmith, Haruna Hirose, James Lee, Jan Fairbairn, Jason Kim, Jay Meistrich, Jeremy Canceko, Jet Harrington, Ji-Young Kim, John Waclawski, Joonwon Kim, Joyce Liong, Karen Holmberg, Kayur Patel, Kenji Ralph Lim, Kenneth Cheng, Lim Jin, Maria Costea, Melo Kalemkeridis, Michael, Michael Eis, Michael Higgins, Mary Jane (MJ) Broadbent, M.J. Chung, Michael Justin Salters, Mickey & Scott Sperlich, Nancy McCarthy, NogginLabs Inc., Paul Pangaro, 小丘, Peter Gassner, Richard P. Gabriel, Richard Price, Richard Tribone, Sam Byun, Sofia Unanue, Sohyoung Choo Ward, Soomin Cho, Stephanie Retz, Steven R. Bible, Sun Kyun Lim, Susan J. Ganz, Taku Wakisaka, Tommy Shek, Woojung Kwon, and Yun Joo Kim.

AT THE PLEDGE LEVEL OF $60 OR MORE: I would like to thank Adam Rotmil, Alan Dickinson, Alexander Cheek, Amena Lee Schlaikjer, Amy C. Park, Andrew Ames, Andrew Newton, Aradhana Goel, Ashley Smith, Bernard Ahn, Caio Avelino, Carla Prinster, Cathy Dekker, Caz Mostowy, Chad McElligott, Chris Smoak, Christopher, Robin Roberts, Daniel Otto Abeshouse, Diane Elizabeth Shrock-Wang, Dj Chuang, Eliot, Hammy Hui, Hyesong Ahn, James Sylvanus, Jenni Merrifield, Jeremy Koempel, Jesse Thomas Gaskin IV, Jill Salahub, Jimmy Chiang, John Duran, Karin Kunori, Kate Hammer, KC Oh, Kenneth Cochanco Go, Brian Kling, Langley Bowers, Larry Seidman, Leslie Fandrich, Lukas Foldyna, Marcelo Aldunce, Mark Graham Dunn, Martin Santiago Salazar, Mary Gordon Hanna, Mia, Michael, Michal Kalousek, Molly Rosenberg, Nico Curtis, Sangmin Lee, Sangwoo Han, SeungBum Kim, Shabihul Abdi, Simon Korzun, Steve Little, Taehee Kim, Richard McLane, Tommy Wang, Tomonori Tsujita, Vincent Kimura, Whitney Hunter-Thomson, Woori Bae, and Brian Wu.

AT THE PLEDGE LEVEL OF $50 OR MORE: I would like to thank Amanda Hennigar, Andrew Ip, Beau Gray, Boo Kim, Boram Yi, Cameron Norman, Cassie Medema, Cath Duncan, Catherine Andreozzi, Chris Coyier, Christopher Ogden, Chuan Liu, Connie Crawford, Curt Sherman, D. Joseph Won, Danny Lam, David Musso, David Xia, Derrick Collins, Kwaku Sefa-Dedeh, Ecem Elci, Edward Lukman, Elaine Ann, Elizabeth Biggs, Field Test Film Corps, Gary Chan, Genevieve Ameduri, Helen Lee, Henry Lin, Hyun Ju Lee, Jae Woo Lee, Joonkoo Park, Kyung Lydia Lee, Lane Vorster, Jason Chen, Jason TS Chiu, Jason Williams, Jeffrey Yan, Jess X. Chen, Jiwon Park, Jocelyn Paige Kelly, Joe Luciani, Joe Sibal, Johannes 'Waldgeist' Rebhan, Jono Lee, Joseph Iloreta, Joonkoo Park, Joseph Shin, Josh Catone, Josh Hartung, Julia Zhu, Julie Song, Jung Ho

347

Park, Jung Hwan Shim, Junko Otake, Justin Chen, Kelly Dahl, Kevin Fox, Kim Korn, Kimberly Shen, Kit Chan, Kyung Lydia Lee, Laurens van de Wiel, Lane Vorster, Lawrence Neeley, Lee Dale, Leslie Fisher, Lisa Orlick, Lois Jones, Lonnie Petersheim, Magda Pecsenye, Marek Belski, Marie-Josée Parent, Mark Busse, Mark Ehrhardt, Matthias Schmitt, Max Orhai, Megan, Mei Ling Chua, Mel Carson, Melissa Rowe, Michael Angeles, Miki DeVivo, Mario Vellandi, Nahyun Kim, Nicolò Volpato, Nitin Sawhney, Olchang, Peter M. Gorys, Peter McKenna, Peter Prip, Philipp Weidhofer, Rolando Brown, Ron Paradis, Rosanne Somerson, Ruby Ku, Sankwon Lew, Sarah Haskell, Sarah Judd Welch, Sean-Joseph Choo, Seho Oh, Shawn Duffy, Shermo, Shilpa Balaji, Sooran, Steve Daniels, Sunny, Susie, Teddy Hahn, Terri Kim, Tim Cheung, Timothy Peck, Todd Sattersten, Tria, Yannick Bertrand, Yijung Noh, Yong Joo Kim, Youngtae Kim, and Yuki Kawae.

AT THE PLEDGE LEVEL OF $25 OR MORE: I would like to thank Ianus Keller, Ah Ra Cho, Andres Lemus, Angela, Anish Ramachandran, Boram Han, Brian Hernandez, Brian Watson, Carla Diana, Carly Ayres, Caroline Choe, Christina Kim, Christine Chun, Chuan-Chun Lai, Cornelia Holden, Deepti Sanghi, EFFALO, Flavia Gnecco, Gwen Oulman Brennan, Hong Qu, Janet McLeod, Jeanne Jo, Jeff Baird, Jennifer Wiebe, Ji Eun Caroline Kim, Joe Hughes, Koo Ho Shin, Lauren Schneider, Marc Noller, Marian Song Park, Merve Karasu, Missy Titus, Anthony Nguyen, R.A. Fedde, Richard Lecours, Rob Stenzinger, Seulgi Kim, Sherry Chang, Sue Kim, Tery Hung, Tim Andonian, and Tom Plaskon.

AT THE PLEDGE LEVEL OF $10 OR MORE: I would like to thank Ashley Mchone, Benjamin Witte, Bill Welense, Bin Davis, Brian Miller, Chris Steib, Connie Wu, Daniel Shiffman, David Del Rosario, Dawa Chung, Elise Nuding, Ellen Ju, Ellie Tripp, Emma Buck, Evelyn Eastmond, George Haines, Hazel Pike, Jack, Jaehoon Chang, James Grady, Jane, Jason Huff, Jean Hazel, JP Reeves, Joo Won Lee, Juan Rafael Lopez, Kyle Cameron Studstill, Kyu, Leslie Leung, Lenora Knowles, Liam Van Vleet, Mark Schenker, Nick Gagalis, Nick Lawrence, Patrick Mulryan, Raul, Rodney Gitzel, SabineM, Sachiko Maruyama, Sandhya Jethnani, Sang Ok, Sang Won Lee, Steve Suhr, Sylvia, Teresa Tan, Tevin Jackson, Thomas Liou, and Wonsik Lee.

AT THE PLEDGE LEVEL OF $1 OR MORE: I would like to thank Ben & Lisa Newton, Eduardas Afanasjevas,

349

Jj Moi, JungHoon Sohn, Matt Johnston, Swarm, Teresa (Horner) Thompson, Vivian Greene, Woven Spaces, Bella Gonzalez, Cynthia Gabriel, Karolle Rabarison, Diana Kimball, Kristie Huey, Mdziedzi, Mukesh, Ravi, Shawna, and Trunksli.

Once again, thank you all for your trust, hope, and love.

Stay beautiful. Always.

351

The first edition of this book has been limited to 1,000 copies, out of which this is no. _662_.

ISBN: 978-0-9858846-0-4